WE ARE HERE FOR YOU

MESSAGES
FROM THE ARCHANGELS
& OTHER
LIGHT BEINGS

To Sissy love always [illegible] my book

Kathleen Peterson

Light Beings Publishing
www.lightbeingsandangels.com

ISBN: 0-9773172-0-X

Design and layout
BBD / Jonathan Gullery
www.budgetbookdesign.com

Manufactured in the United States of America

Dedication

This book is dedicated to the Archangels and Other Light Beings, with gratitude for sharing their love and wisdom in this work. It couldn't have been written without you.

Acknowledgements

So many people contributed to the publishing of this book. I wish to thank two people who have been very important in my Spiritual Development. Louise Taylor my first spiritual teacher, who was instrumental in awakening me to the Divine Spirit within and did an amazing job of guiding me along the path. Thanks also to Doreen Virtue PhD who willingly and graciously shares her gifts with the world and encourages others to do the same. Thanks for giving me the support and the courage to step out into the world and acknowledge I am a lightworker.

Special thanks goes to Valerie Camozzi whose friendship, support and numerous nudging got this book published. I am grateful for all she did, even her file to keep me on track. Thanks to Leanda Duncan for sharing the vision and getting this set up in the early stages. To my Annapolis spiritual friends Terry Oliver, Louise Nue, Susan Rudolph, Kathy Braithewaite, and Kay Powell thanks for the monthly encouragement, meditation and spiritual conversation. To Kay Sharp, Carol Meadows, Sheila Sellers and everyone at the Healing Arts Center, those Monday nights were always an inspiration and a spiritual haven. To my friends in Virginia, Maggie Crossgrove, Jill Johnston, Jim Mattox and Elena Romanova the dinners, laughter and support helped me through some difficult times.

Thanks also to my family for their support and encouragement including, Gen and Harvey Peterson, Jim Peterson, Lee and Nona Peterson, Fern and Morgan O'Brien.

My gratitude knows no bounds to the Archangels and Other Light Beings. Without you there would be no book. You are the book. I am merely your scribe.

Introduction

This book began when I was meditating, in February 2004. It was during meditation that I was asked to channel messages from the archangels and ascended masters and to send these messages to others. It was from these messages that the book began. I have taken the first 101 messages and put them into book form.

The idea behind the book is to bring these messages to people, so that they may know that they are not alone. Spiritual beings from the other realms are offering support and love.

This book is to be read randomly. Take a deep breath, go within and ask, "What is the message for the day?" After you have asked the question, let the book open to whichever angel or enlightened being has your message for the day. As I have discovered each day, the angel or ascended master (enlightened being) that comes through me has a message specifically for others and me.

I am grateful and honored to be the channel for these messages. The words and style are "those of the angels and other enlightened beings" who send them. I am merely the means by which they are manifested onto paper. These messages are for you, the reader, sent with love to give encouragement and support as you go through your daily life. They are one way to let you know that you are not alone and all you have to do is "ask." Help is on the way!

Kathleen Peterson

Contents

One

Archangel Michael

I am here to tell all of you that it is time to awaken and work from your soul. Look deep into yourselves for answers, as you have all knowledge inside of you. You are bright stars and it is time, as you have all been told, to let your light shine. We understand that some of you doubt that there is any light there at all, but trust us when we say that your beings are full of very bright light and now is the time to let it shine! I tell you that as you move forward into your own, you will have all the help you need from all of us. We stand by to help with any questions or situations that need clarification or healing.

Each of you committed to come into this life to fulfill your role in transforming the earth plane, from one of fear to one of love and trust, both in one another and in the universal wisdom. I come to you today to give you my promise that I am here to help you with courage, releasing negative thoughts and energy and also to protect and guide, whenever I am asked to do so.

As you go through your day today, think of the graceful power that is within you and know that that power is one of love. You have been gifted to share that love with others so that they, too, can see the love within themselves. Let your love shine out from within, without fear. Know that a smile or a gentle touch for someone can help ease much pain, both within you and others. I see such joy lying deep within the heart of each of you, that when you tap into it you will be amazed that it has been there all along, merely covered by thoughts of fear and doubt about what you deserve. Know that you deserve love, light, laughter, prosperity and joy. It is all around you and you can manifest it by focusing on what you want in your life rather than what you fear.

I thank each and every one of you for reading this message and send blessings and love as you go through this day. See the love within and let it shine forth today!

Two

Isis

I come to you today to talk of being gentle with yourselves. As you move through your day it is time to give yourselves uplifting messages about every step you take. Too many of you have been taught that to make a mistake is terrible and you forget that this is the way to learn. Remember how it was when you were a small child and you began to walk. Every time you fell it gave you a better idea about what to do to avoid falling the next time. Do not be afraid of the mistakes that you make. Know that they are mere steps to carry you further along your path. They are like the corrections that put you back in the right direction. Celebrate each step. Do not judge the size of the triumph or the type. See each one as a movement toward your goal or toward your life purpose.

You are wonderful beings who have chosen to come into the earth plane at this time. You can call on me to help you feel better about yourselves. I will help you see the glory that is you. I will help you open to the power, strength, grace and poise that already exist within just waiting for you to uncover it.

Whenever you are facing something and are unsure if you can face it, call on me to help you. I will be standing behind you, spreading my wings to help expand your strength and grace. Know that I will come when you call for me, to aid you with your life's challenges.

Again I emphasize, be gentle with yourself. Be kind and joyfully face each day and each task. The more that you thank yourself and celebrate each action the more you will see things in a positive light. Each action you take gives you strength to go to the next thing. Celebrate yourself and your lives!

I thank you for reading this and asking me to be part of your lives on this earth plane.

Three

Archangel Haniel

I come to you today to help you connect with the divine magic within you. You all have the ability to tap into this magic and if you are unsure how to do so, call on me and listen as I help you make the connection. This connection can help you manifest and create miracles in your life. Just ask, listen and trust that you have the ability to do this. I also help with speaking, so when you find yourselves in a situation that requires tact and social skills, call on me and as the song says, "I'll be there" (just a little humor for the day).

I wish to speak of the fear many of you have that the world, as you know it, is descending into hell. I have worked with humanity forever and have seen the changes that are taking place here and now. I am here to tell you that there is more good than evil. For every act of terror and hate, there are hundreds of acts of kindness and healing. Know that your world is rising up in an attitude of love. I know that it doesn't always look that way from your position, but from my position seeing everything, I see an increase in the feeling of love and caring among your fellow humans.

I leave you with the thought to "look for the good" in each, and you will be rewarded by the manifestation of that good; the more good you see, the more will be created! Remember your divine magic!

I thank you for reading this and send blessings and light to each.

Four

Archangel Raguel

I am the Archangel who oversees all of the angels, to help to keep harmony and be there for them. My dears, I am here today to let you know you are not asking for help from us often enough. It saddens me to see so many of you trying to do everything on your own when there are so many around who are waiting to help if you will just ask. One of my main roles is to be there for all of you whenever you ask for help. I will listen and give you ideas about what to do.

Some have referred to me as a "best friend." I am here for you as are all of the angels and ascended masters. Remember time, space or physical bodies do not confine us. We can be in many places at once and assist all at the same time. We can't assist if you don't ask. Know that you are not alone and that we are here for you. Grant us the opportunity to help you and smooth some of the issues you face. We will not interfere as you have choice, but we can bring fresh ideas and we can help you to manifest positive events and physical realities in your lives.

I thank you for reading this message and I wish to leave you with one thought. "Ask, ask, ask!" Know we will respond and know that you are not alone.

I thank you for reading this message and send you blessings, love, and light.

Five

Abundantia

I come to you today to remind all that your prosperity comes from the source. It doesn't originate from your job, your project or even your spiritual works.

I ask you to call on me when you have questions about your finances and during your dreamtime I will answer the questions. I invite you to call on me to bring you unexpected sources of money.

I ask you to trust that I will be there to help you release any fears or worries about finances and security. When you focus your energy on the money you don't have, this continues to bring you more of the same. I offer the idea that the more gratitude you show for everything, the more that will come your way.

For those of you who like concrete things to do I will provide an exercise that will increase your prosperity. On Sunday of each week state, "This week I will experience a miracle having to do with money." As you go through your week, if you find any money on the street, in your pocket or via the mail, express your gratitude with great joy and then say, "This week I will experience more miracles having to do with money." I can say that this is a very powerful exercise and know that you will find it beneficial. I leave you with this idea.

Call on me for help and I will come, bringing unexpected resources and gifts. Also, change your focus to one of faith and knowing that you will be taken care of financially and that you deserve "the all."

Thank you for your loving attention to my message and I send you blessings and joy.

Six

Forseti

I will work behind the scenes to assist you with any disputes, especially legal ones. I am here today to assist you in settling any and all arguments so they become a win for each party. I bring peace to all concerned.

I will come when you call for protection in all legal matters, including the signing of contracts. I come immediately to your side, so that these issues can be resolved quickly and equitably. I am here for you, so you can move from a state of mind of obsessing and concern to one of knowing that all will be resolved for the highest good of all concerned. I can be of assistance in issues which are not legal, but personal. I look for truth and peace. Call on me to assist along with your angels and others, both of the earth plane and the spiritual realm.

I send blessings and thank you for reading this message. It is important to know that even though my message may not be of importance to you today, I may be of assistance in the future so know I am here.

Seven

Archangel Metatron

I come to you today to offer encouragement to all of you to move forward in your life. Give your fear of success and failure to the angels and to me. We want only joy and peace for all. Again I repeat what you have heard before, "watch your thoughts, for energy flows where attention goes!"

You can control what you think. Just stop and check where your thoughts are headed. If you find yourselves staying in fear, check your thoughts and if you have to say Stop! Use the word several times and turn your thoughts to positive ones. I hear all of you saying "easier said than done", but I say to you that once you begin consciously focusing your thoughts on what you want instead of what you fear, you will begin to reap the rewards for which you all work so hard.

Call on me to help keep you focused on the positive. Call on me to help motivate you to step boldly into your life and to help you follow your dreams. I am here to say everything is possible, even changing your beliefs to support the wonderful beings that you are. Too many of you fail to realize the grandness of who you are. It is time to declare that you are wonderful and deserve abundance, joy and peace.

I will help you with your self-worth issues, giving you ideas and suggestions to use to move forward in your life. I leave you with the idea that you are deserving of all the good and joy and abundance that the universe can provide and as you know, the universe is limitless. Go forth with joy in your hearts, knowing that as you go through your day you touch everyone with your energy. How your energy goes out is up to you. Joy and peace beget joy and peace. Be bold, be fearless and be the strength that you are.

I thank you for reading this message and send you blessings and love.

Eight

Archangel Metatron

I come today to tell you to call on me when you need to be motivated to step boldly forward and toward what you want. I tell you to call on me for motivation to move in the proper direction, without fear of reprisal or that you may be going in the wrong direction. If you have questions, ask and I will provide ideas and inspiration to help you along your path.

Release your fears of not being worthy to me and I will transform them into feelings of strength and security. Know that you are worthy of all the abundance, joy and peace that the universe offers. Spirit and the angels desire only that which is joyful for you. Many of you doubt your worth and focus on lack and fear that you will be penniless. I come to tell you this is in your mind and that it is time to focus your thoughts on the positive! Your minds are very powerful and you have let them have control. It is now time for you to realize that you are more than your mind and you can control it. Call on me and I will help you move forward and focus positively.

I send you love. Know you are love and light. Know in your hearts that you are worthy and deserve all the abundance and joy and peace the universe, which is limitless, has to offer.

Release the fear and ask the angels to help.

Call on me to motivate and encourage you to follow your dream, because dreams are a way that Spirit sets you on the path to your joy. Step boldly forth and light the way for others to follow.

I give thanks to you for reading this message and send blessings and love.

Nine

Archangel Gabriel

⁀◟◞

I come to you in love and joy. It is time to let your creative side out into the light. Many of you are speakers, writers and artists, although you have not done much with any of it because of the outrageously high standards you set for yourselves. Allow that which is within you to come forth. You all have creative abilities and I am here to offer my assistance in any way you wish.

Open your minds, hearts and souls to the joyful creativity within you. Give yourselves free reign to do whatever feels right about expressing yourselves. Opening to creativity leads to new ideas about life, work and play. Unleash the creative power within you! As you move through your day let the images that are around you enter your being and then translate these images into music, art or writing.

For those of you who will be speaking, I am here to open doors and smooth the way. Many of you will be giving talks before groups. Call on me to assist with any and all creative endeavors.

I am here to tell you that each of you has the creative ability inside of you. Do not compare yourselves to others, as you are each unique and valuable. I am strong and helpful. Call on me whenever you need help with speaking your truth, expressing yourself, or you need ideas about moving forward in your career. I can guide you along the way, just remember to listen.

I leave you with this idea: You are wonderful, valuable individuals who need to give yourselves encouragement in every way. I will stand with you to encourage your growth and your joy. Be joyful as you move through your life, for joy begets joy.

I thank you and send you blessings. Just call on me when you need assistance. I join all the angels awaiting your requests to smooth your way.

Ten

Quan Yin

I come to you today to let you know that you are all valuable and wonderful. We see all that you do to live your lives in peace and harmony, giving to those in need either financially or by listening and helping in other ways. Your compassion for others is wonderful. It is time, however, that you show the same compassion for yourselves.

You are all living your lives to the best of your abilities and I give you love and approval for all that you do. You are in need of your own approval. Slow down and take a look at all you have done throughout your lives! Give yourself approval for everything, each step you take, every day you step out and face life on the earth plane.

I see many of you rushing to succeed, rushing to create financial prosperity, hoping that with all of your efforts it will finally happen. I wish to tell you to slow down. Listen to the angels and listen to the ascended masters. You all ask for help and then don't take the time to listen. Allow things to come to you, slow down and you will see that life can be beautiful and abundant as you allow things to be delivered, rather than chasing them and trying to force the issues. Grant yourselves the opportunity to enjoy that which you already possess. You are all beautiful; I know that you have all heard this before!

Call on me whenever you doubt or fear. I will come to help, as Mary, the mother, comes. I am available to all to help with problems and to help to open your eyes to beauty around you.

As you go through your day today take the time to listen to those you have asked for help. Affirm that all good things are now being delivered to you. You deserve grace and blessings. Learn to slow down and accept these things into your life. Life will open before you, as the lotus flower opens to the sun.

I thank you for your attention and send you blessings.

Eleven

Dana

Greetings, I thank you for inviting me to speak to you today. I continue along the same lines as those who have come before me.

I wish to let you know that you are all royalty and, as such, have great powers and gifts. You all came into the earth plane, at this time, to bring positive messages of hope, joy, laughter and light. You have come to help change the energy, from one of fear to one of glory and peace. You all have the ability to create magic and alchemy. You can look inside yourselves to realize the power you have.

Treat yourselves as kings and queens! Realize that you deserve the all of the universe. Realize that you have the ability to create and manifest that which you desire. Abundance, joy and happiness are yours for the asking. I am here to guide and support you, as you move forward in your life. Call on me to assist you with issues of abundance, feelings of self-worth and self-esteem. I can guide and direct you to see yourself in a new light.

Live from your heart and know that your heart is loving and good. Know that the powers that you have are strong and loving and that whenever you use them, you do so for the highest good of all.

I leave you with this thought for the day: You are all royalty and are each deities in your own right. If you look to the words of Jesus, you will know that he taught that what he could do each of you can do or something greater. His message confirms that you are all equal to him in every way. Do not fear this, but look to it with joy knowing that when you change your beliefs about yourselves, you can change what happens in your life. You are capable of great things!

I give you blessings and thanks for reading this message.

Twelve

Ganesh

I bring you blessings from Spirit and say that I am here to remove any and all obstacles in your path. Many of you create obstacles to prevent yourselves from moving forward. These are illusions that can easily be removed with or without my help.

When you project fear into the future, you create obstacles that will block any movement and help to keep you stuck just where you are. I tell you that you are not always conscious of the obstacles you create and you believe that they are created without your help! Call on me and I will remove the obstacles, so that you can look at the now and at the future with hope and faith that everything is working for your highest good.

Focus your thoughts on the positive and ask for help to remove the fear. Living in fear does you no good and worry never solved a problem. I am here to walk in front of you with love and wisdom, which will remove many of the doubts and fears that invade your souls. Trust that I can remove these things and smooth your way, so that you can walk in the light toward the brightness that awaits you today and tomorrow.

Know that the illusions, which are created as obstacles, are not necessarily created on a conscious level. Call on me and I will be there to remove that which is blocking you from being the best you can be.

I leave you with this thought for the day: Obstacles are merely the way you keep yourselves from moving forward and taking your rightful place to share wisdom, love and light on the earth plane. Call on me to remove obstacles and help you focus your thoughts on abundance, love and knowing that everything is possible.

I send you much love and thank you for reading this message.

Thirteen

Archangel Zadkiel

∽

I bring you love and forgiveness messages today. I come before you to help with any feelings of unforgiveness you have for yourself or others. I will assist with all feelings that hurt you. It is important to forgive both yourself and others. The power of anger you carry toward either only hurts you. The ability to forgive the person, yet not the act that was done, is what I am here to help you with.

All humans can get caught up in emotional moments and say or do unkind things leaving you with anger and hurt, although you are probably the most unforgiving toward yourself. I am here today, which is a day on your earth plane of love, to tell you I will help you release any issues about forgiveness. I will help you release your soul of the feelings of hurt and anger you have carried for many decades, some of which you are unaware. Go into your quiet space today and call on me to help you release these feelings. We will work together to do this gently. Know that once these feelings have been released you will feel lighter and more in harmony with everything.

I also come to you today to ask that you drop all judgment of yourself. Forgive and know that you are doing and saying what you think is right, given what information you have. We know that you come from a place of love and caring; and rather than judge, call on me to help you send blessings of love and light to the behavior or statement. Know that I will help you to see yourself with love and understanding, rather than judgment.

Today is a day for you to treat yourself with love and care. Give yourself a treat! Do something special for yourself. You are always giving to others, today give to yourself. Have a body treatment, or go to a movie, or walk in nature and give thanks and appreciation for the wonder that is you. All of us see you as wonderful and loving. Know that you are all wonderful, lovable beings struggling to live in human form according to contracts you made prior to incarnating. Today Heal, Celebrate and Love YOU. We do.

I thank you for reading this message and I send blessings, light and love.

Fourteen

Babaji

I come to you today to reinforce your faith. I want you to know that whatever path you choose to connect with Spirit, it is the correct path for you. No one person has the only path to connection. You are already connected. It is a matter of awakening to the spirit within.

I come to tell you that if you call on me, I will help you with the connection. You don't need me, as you already have a direct connection, but you doubt that you are connected. I will assist you in opening your heart to the connection that lies within. Once the connection is made to your satisfaction, you can always call on me to increase the connection.

Once you open your heart to the spirit within, you will be amazed at the miracles which can occur. The closer the connection you feel, the more serenity you will have, as all things come with the knowledge that you are connected, not only with Spirit, but with everyone and everything.

You are all divine and it is important to honor the divine within. I tell you that when you awaken and begin to listen to the divine guidance from within, your lives will change. You will honor the loving power that is you. Everything will become clear and you will see things from a different perspective.

Call on me to help you awaken to your connection with the divine. Talk to Spirit and listen for the answers, as the answers are there.

I leave you with this thought. Call on me to increase your awareness of the connection with Spirit, but know that you are already connected and you only need to open your heart to hear the answers to questions. You are divine.

I thank you for reading this message and send you love, light and blessings from all who are here to help you along your path.

Fifteen

Aphrodite

I come today to bring you blessings and let you know that now is the time to strengthen your relationship with your partner. I will come to help you increase the passion and understanding in your relationship.

To have a successful love relationship you need both passion and understanding. With the combination, you move beyond the friendship connection and into a bonding that can only be experienced by this relationship between two people. Call on me to help with this.

You are all loving, caring beings and when you connect with another in this combination, then your life will take on another dimension. This is not to say that this is necessary for a complete life, it is just another connection and one that can help to open your heart. I can aid you in this when you ask.

I also come today to speak of the beauty that is within each of you. Many of you see faults and defects and I tell you that to those of us on the other planes you are beautiful. Each of you has a distinct and individual beauty that, as you grow in your connection to your higher-self and Spirit, comes through to the outer limits of your physical self. That is when those around you can see the beauty that is you.

It is time for you to see the beauty that is you and change your focus from looking at your sags, bags and wrinkles and look for the beauty that is you.

I will help you see your beauty. I will help you focus on the you that is perfect, within and without. I come to help you accept yourself as you. The more that you accept and love yourself with the same passion and understanding that you would look for in a relationship, the more you will connect with Spirit and others. Know that this is important to healthy living both in spirit and in the physical world.

I leave you with this thought: You are all, beautiful and now is the time for you to love yourself with passion and understanding. I will help you with this.

With the dawn of each new day, affirm that you are beautiful just as you are and you deserve all the passion and understanding that is in the universe. Accept this passion and understanding as your due.

I send you blessings and love and thank you for reading this message.

Sixteen

Diana

I bring you blessings and support from all of us in the other realms. I am here today to tell you to let the light that is within you shine forth. Your soul wishes to be all that you are.

Do not fear ridicule, criticism or any other judgments from others. It is you, with the help of divine guidance, who knows what is best for you. You are unique and as such are a valuable part of the whole.

You are needed at this time to be that part of the whole that you committed to before you came to the earth plane. Do not hide your light out of fear, as it does not benefit anyone. You have all been told this before but I am here to reinforce all you have been told about allowing your light to shine. Rise above your fear and Be all that you can be!

What you are is much greater than what you currently see. Allow yourself to rejoice in the wonder that is you. Now is the time! Your all is needed to complete the whole. The more you can come from your authentic self and shine the light of the divine from within, the more that you contribute to the earth plane.

Call on me to help you rise above problems in your life,

which are bogging you down and clouding your light. Come into your own! Be bright, be light, be love and be here now! You have much to offer and you chose to come into the earth plane at this time to help with the shifting vibrations. You are needed.

I will help you to move out and up, so that you may view your life from a different perspective. Give me your trust and I will show you the beauty that is you. Do not hesitate to open to the power and light that is within you. Know that the more you accept who you are the more powerful you are, because then you will not be influenced by other's judgment of you and you will release the fear which holds you in place.

I am here for you, as is Spirit and all of the angels and ascended masters. Do not hesitate to call on us to help you with anything. The more you can let go of the struggle and accept the help, the more you can release the fear. Call on us!

I thank you for reading this message and send you much love and light. May the beauty that is around you and in you fill each of your days.

Seventeen

Archangel Zadkiel

I come today to help you heal the unforgiveness in your hearts. It is time to release all of those feelings of unforgiveness toward yourself or others. It is time for you to step into the light without the burdens you carry of anger, hate and judgment. These emotions are OK as long, as you realize that you can release them.

It is part of your human struggle to deal with these emotions. Many of you hold onto your anger feeling justified, because the treatment you received was unnecessary and undeserved. I ask that you think about the idea that the only one who feels this burden of unforgiveness is you. I will help you lift these feelings, so that you will emerge lighter and more open to the exciting opportunities which await you.

I know that you feel you have a right to be angry and hurt, but it is important to realize that if you can be willing to release these feelings toward another or toward yourself, you will begin to feel more optimistic. I am not asking you to accept the behavior, but to realize that the person behind the behavior is coming from whatever is happening in her/his life. Sometimes you become the focus of the frustration, because you can be trusted to accept the person regardless of the behavior. Take care of yourself and forgive the behavior. I will help you sweep this out of your life.

I do not suggest you should stay in any situation which creates pain for you, but once you have done what is important for you then it is time to release the feelings rather than hang onto them. You deserve the best, both from yourselves and others. When situations arise which create feelings of anger, hurt and discomfort, call on me to smooth the way and help you do or say what is best for all concerned.

I know that sometimes it is difficult to release the feelings of unforgiveness. Just be willing! The key word is willing. The longer you hold onto feelings of anger and unforgiveness the greater the chances these feelings will affect your physical being, so be willing to release. Even if you are unsure of what the problem is, I will help you release any old feelings gently and smoothly. You don't always have to be aware of what is keeping you stuck or in pain to release it. Just ask for my help to release any and all feelings of unforgiveness toward yourself, others or any old situations and it will be done.

You can ask for help as many times as you feel it is necessary to clear things up for yourself. Remember, the important person in this is you! The more you can release any and all of these feelings the better it will be for you. It will not affect others at all. You are important to the all and I repeat what you have heard before, "Now is the time to step into your power and light, so release!"

I thank you for reading this message and I send healing, blessings and love.

Eighteen

Isis

I come to you today to speak of honoring the divine feminine within. Man or woman, you each have the divine feminine within. It is appropriate that I come to speak to you today, as it is the time of the new moon, and the feminine is connected with the moon.

It is time to acknowledge the importance of the divine feminine on the earth plane at this time. This is a time when, as you know, there is a rapid emergence of the divine feminine. It is right that this is so.

The energy is shifting, so that there will be a balance between the masculine and the feminine. At this point, your earth has been under the rule of the masculine, aggressive energy. As the feminine energy becomes stronger, you will notice a shift in the way that things are done. There will be more working together in a spirit of cooperation. People will become more inclined to reach some kind of consensus.

I am here today to help you honor that part of yourself. I am here to demonstrate to all, the grace, poise and confidence, which can come from the feminine. I come to share your joy in being able to connect with that which is within you and to help you bring this forth and manifest it into the physical. Look to me and I will show you the way of strength and joy.

You are all shifting into a time when you will accomplish more by allowing your feminine side to lead the way, rather than the old way of aggression and demands. This is not to say that you will be, as you say, weak, but that by your very ability to see all points of view and to desire the best for everyone, your very strength will come forth. Call on me to show you the way! Call on me to lead you toward the strength of the divine feminine within. I will hear and answer your call.

We all stand with you and share in the shift of energy. Remember, by allowing the shift, by expressing more of the feminine energy, you help to shift the energy of the earth plane and as you shift this energy you affect everyone and everything. It is time!

Go forth in all your beauty and allow the new moon of today to help you step more fully into the divine feminine, which is already within. You are loved and needed, now!

I thank you for reading this message and I send you love, nurturing and blessings as you move through your life.

Nineteen

Quan Yin

❦

I come today to speak to you about compassion, both for yourselves and others. As you grow within your spirit, you will begin to see that everyone is on their own path toward enlightenment and connection with Spirit.

As each struggles to live life on the earth plane, many will make painful mistakes. I can help ease this pain by assisting in your ability to look at these mistakes with compassion. Although it is not always easy to stand in another's footprints, it can be done, so that if something is said or done and you feel hurt by it, with the compassion of the heart, you can see that it comes from another's pain. Have compassion for yourself as well.

I am here to repeat, that you are all too demanding and critical of yourselves! Show compassion to yourself as well, so that when mistakes are made, you can grow and learn from them, rather than feel stupid, depressed, or guilty. Many of you are quite good at showing compassion to others, now turn it toward yourselves; you are as deserving of it as others! You are traveling your path and learning, the same as everyone.

I ask that you see yourselves from a broader perspective

and know that all of us, in other realms, are supporting you as you travel through your human experience.

I leave you with this today: Call on me to help with your path. I will come to love you and show you compassion. I will help you to learn to show compassion toward yourself, so that you can move to another level in your awakening. Listen for my response to your questions; I will always come when you call. You are on the path to enlightenment; waking up to the spiritual being you are now.

I thank you for reading this and send you compassion, blessings and much love. Let me help light the way.

Twenty

Abundantia

⟨❀⟩

I come to you, today, to talk about the abundance of the universe and to reinforce that this abundance is available to all. Many of you give all of your energy to the fear that you will not have enough to meet your needs. Remember, what you focus on is where the energy flows and if the energy flows toward fear of "lack", that is what will continue to flow into your life.

I can help you accept the abundance that is yours for the asking. I can help you with you issues surrounding success and prosperity. Picture me with coins flowing from my hands into yours, assisting you with success and prosperity. Many of you are afraid to ask for help. Many of you are afraid to believe that you deserve abundance and prosperity. I come to you today to tell you to raise your eyes and your sights. You deserve the best! You deserve to partake in the abundance of the universe. Know that what you focus on, with intention, will flow to you easily and effortlessly. I understand that from a human perspective this is difficult to believe. If you have to, suspend your belief that you have to work hard for your money in order to ask for prosperity and expect that your request will be granted, then do so. Imagine, that whatever your need, it will be met and more will come to you. Call on me and I will help you visualize, with feeling, that you needs are being met now; that you have more than you need and that what you receive, has exceeded your expectations. Set your sights higher and experience the joy of manifesting, with the help of Spirit, all that you need and more!

As you know, your source for prosperity is Spirit. Suspend your belief that you will not have enough. Take my hand I will help you! Focus your mind and your thoughts on the idea that everything you need is here and is manifesting in your life now. Change that belief of "lack"! Sever all vows of poverty that you took throughout many lifetimes. You are worthy, you are powerful, you are deserving. Remember whatever you can imagine you can manifest. Call on me to show you the way! I love to help with issues of abundance. I appreciate your gratitude for the abundance as it arrives. Watch your thoughts and cancel every doubt about your ability to manifest prosperity. Be vigilant and change your thoughts, from doubt to knowing you are prosperous! I will help. Just ask! Give me your fear and doubt and I will transmute it into love and help you to refocus your thought.

I send you great love and many blessings. I shower you with thoughts of prosperity and joy.

Twenty-One

Archangel Raphael

Greetings! I bring you love and healing through every part of your life! I come to you today to talk about the healer within. You are all God made manifest and therefore, you are capable of great things, including healing. Know that when you call on me to help with healing I will come, but in essence I am helping to facilitate your healing from within. I will come when called, to help with healing for yourself or anyone you want to help with healing.

I am one of the better known archangels and this is because I work closely with Archangel Michael. Call on me to help you with any type of healing. Know, however, that when you call on me to heal someone other than yourself I can go to that person, but I cannot interfere in their process unless I am asked by them! I will, however, bring my energy of care and comfort to help.

When you call on me to help you, I can actually assist in your healing. Trust that your request is being answered whenever you ask. It is important for you to know that I will come at any time. I can assist in releasing old lower energies, to help you open up to deeper communication with Spirit.

I am also compelled to tell you that, as an archangel, I am a messenger from God, but you do not have to communicate with Spirit through me. You can have direct communication with Spirit! In truth, God would like you to talk to her/him more often.

Look to the divine within you to open the connection with the universal divine wisdom and love. Continue to call on all of us from Spirit, but never forget your own, immediate connection with Spirit. Your connection is real and you are heard. Take the time to listen as Spirit does respond!

As you go about your busy day, take the time to give gratitude to the divine! This will help with healing more than anything that I can do. Keep your avenues of communication open and let your hearts fill with the love, as it flows through and to you.

I thank you for reading this message and send you waves of bright emerald green light to surround, fill and bring you healing.

Twenty-Two

Archangel Michael

I come today to talk to you about courage. You are all profoundly gifted, both in your connection to Spirit and in your connection in the earth plane. It is time to release the doubt about your gifts, be they involved in working within the structures of the earth plane or working with Spirit. Whenever you doubt, call on me and I will assist you in gathering your courage to step out and let the world know your gifts!

It is time for all of you to take your courage in hand and step out. Let your gifts go to work! Let your light shine, so that others may learn to shine theirs. You are powerful and must be willing to come forth with all that you are capable of doing. I can see your hesitation and hear the doubts that lie in your hearts. Do not be afraid! The earth plane is waiting for you.

You agreed before you came into this life that this time, you would use your gifts. Call on me and I will assist you in any way you request. Be strong, and step out! Let your gifts be put to use for the good of all. Some may think I speak only of gifts of Spirit, but I speak to those of you involved in what some would call "worldly projects." All are needed. I will assist all, as everything is connected to Spirit.

You are here to share your knowledge and wisdom. You are here to help lead the way for others, to make this earth a better place, filled with joy, laughter, and peace for everyone. Take your courage in your hand and go forth and share the information and caring you committed to share! Do not wait! Do not be afraid of ridicule, criticism or rejection, I will help you through this and you have much more support than you are aware of, both from Spirit and on the earth plane. You are needed NOW! If you are unsure of exactly what you are to do, listen to your heart. Ask for information and listen for the answer; you will recall why you are here! Have courage and know that this is what you are meant to do. Come, spread your wings and fly! Whenever things become too frightful, call on me to help you.

I send you love and courage to step forward and use the profound gifts, with which you incarnated into this life. Blessings and joy as each day progresses! I am here for you any time, anywhere.

Twenty-Three

Damara

I come to you today to offer my help with manifesting abundance and harmony in your home. Know that you have the right to have harmony in your home, and with those who share your home. I will help with this. Call on me and I will go to those in conflict to create non-judgment and understanding. I can help to create a peaceful atmosphere, so that you have serenity. I can help you release your fear and judgment toward those who share your home, just ask. It is important to release judgment of others, so that you can look at them with an open heart.

Each of you is walking your own path and each path is as unique as the person walking it. As you know, there are many things that you each think and do differently from one another. It is important to know that each is appropriate for the individual. Unless there is pain and hurt by statements or actions, then it is best to let things be.

Call on me to help with issues of forgiveness towards one another. I can come to everyone involved and show the way to release judgment, criticism and any other emotion that can harm you or another, regardless of who is sending the emotion. If you are in judgment and anger, I can help you let it go and transmute it into love; if it comes from someone else, I can go to them and whisper in their ear, asking for non-judgment and understanding, which will help with the situation.

I am also here to help with abundance in your home. I will help with manifesting anything needed to create serenity in your home, be it help with the monthly payment or money to fix it up. Just ask and I will help you release feelings of lack and fear about continuing to live in your home in comfort. I will help you as often as necessary to help you manifest abundance.

Know that you are all powerful and can release feelings of lack and move into feelings of abundance surrounding your home. Shift your focus and feel the abundance intensely and it will be manifested.

I thank you for reading this message and send you abundance and harmony in your home.

Twenty-Four

Dana

Today, I come to talk with you about receiving. It is time for you to receive. You all know how to give and you think you know how to receive, but I tell you that most of you put obstacles in your way when it comes to receiving. I will help you with this.

I am honored to serve you and to treat you as the royalty that you are. When will you accept that which is yours? When will you allow Spirit to give to you, without fear that you are deserving?

As we have discussed before, you are all deities in your own right. You are Spirit made manifest and as such, are capable of creating divine miracles, always! You know, somewhere in your hearts, that you are capable of manifesting, but when you begin to manifest you seem to hesitate and then you create something which prevents the manifestation. This is not a conscious thought.

I tell you, that you deserve all that the universe has to offer. You are worthy of all that you can dream of. It is time to open your hearts and minds and accept the gifts that you desire. Call on me to help you set your doubts aside, so that you can receive that which you work to manifest.

See yourself as divine and royal, even if it is for a brief moment. Sit and allow yourself to feel and imagine the royalty that you are and give gratitude for the glorious things that are being delivered to you.

Imagine that you sit with a crown on your head and everything you desire is being delivered to you now. Feel what that is like! I know that even in this situation, some of you will place what you call qualifiers, or limits. Be open in this situation, even if it is only for a minute, because in that minute, you will have some idea of who you really are. Receive without reservation! Use your skills to manifest and then allow yourself to receive that which you have manifested.

I can hear many of you saying that "What is manifested must be spiritual", however, I say to you, "It can be of this world!" Do not block things, such as a fancy car or home, just because you believe that they are not spiritual.

Everything is from Spirit and all are energy. You are all capable of divine magic! Believe that you deserve it and then create and receive. I will assist you as you move through this process. I am honored to serve you and wish to help you receive the joy, laughter and gifts that are here for you. Open your hearts, put your doubts aside and receive with open arms and no qualifications. You are divine!

I thank you for reading this message and send blessings of joy, laughter and lightness into your hearts today. Hail to you!!

Twenty-Five

Maat

I come today to continue your connection to your divine power. I tell you that you are connected with the moon and the cycles of the moon affect all, whether male or female. When you are younger, you will feel these affects more strongly, but as you age the connection remains strong. The moon has been said to connect with the female aspect of humanity and this is true.

It is important that all become more aware of their feminine traits. Spend some time with the moon. See how the ebb and flow of you follows the ebb and flow of the moon. Check in with yourself at the time of the full moon and the new moon. Differentiate between the two, as they carry vary different characteristics and affect you in very different ways. The moon adds to your power. I am here to offer my help in this connection and the divine magic that your connection with the moon produces. You have much divine magic to produce. Follow your heart and ask to use your powers to produce this divine magic.

The moon can help you become more aware of your abilities and how these abilities connect with the divine feminine within. Do not fear your power, as it is from love and will be used to aid and provide for those in need of guidance and nurturing. I will help you look inside with truth and integrity. Open your eyes and your hearts and feel the connection with the moon, as it is connected to the seas and within the universe. There is power there. Become more aware of it and the gifts you have because of this connection. You will be amazed at what will occur when you acknowledge this connection.

I thank you for reading this message and send you love, truth, integrity and blessings.

Twenty-Six

Athena

I come to you today to speak of strength and wisdom. I am a warrior and protector. You, too, can be a warrior and protector, but do as I do and use your intuition when you engage. Do not be concerned about physical strength, you have the power within. Go inside and listen to what comes from your inner connection with the Divine. That is where your strength and power lie. You may call on me to assist you in standing in your power and strength. Your intuition will assist you in any confrontation.

Know that you have the wisdom to move and protect in any situation. I can demonstrate how you, too, can stand in your warrior self and yet be loving and peaceful. It is important for you to know today that you are strong and wise. You are capable of using everything around you to support your beliefs. Everything is energy and as such, can be controlled by connection. Be aware that what you ask for and intend can be accomplished with the help of the energetic forces around you. Go inside to the wisdom which lies there and use that wisdom to assist you in everything. The only caution I give is to be aware of your focus, for what you focus on, via thought or feeling, will be sent to the universe and returned to you. You are powerful and strong. I come before you to protect and assist in helping you to develop your strength without fear. Stand tall, walk with confidence and speak your truth with love and integrity, for when you come from the divine connection within and you use the energies of the earth and cosmos for the highest good, then you will succeed. Stand strong, yet flexible using the wisdom from within to guide, protect and direct you in everything you do.

Know you are powerful and affect many things with your thoughts and intentions. Wear your power with care and understanding, so that you look to the highest good for all. You must use your power for your highest good, which will, in turn, help those around you. You deserve consideration. Use the power within to assist you as you seek to succeed.

I thank you for reading this message and I stand ready to protect and serve you as you progress on the earth plane. The stars and I salute you and say, "Call on us and use our energy to assist. You are loved!"

Twenty-Seven

Saint Germain

I come to you today to talk about what it means to be a light-worker. Many of you know that you are light-workers, yet there are those among you who are probably saying, "Who me?" I say to you that you are all light-workers. I know because you are in receipt of this message.

There are no coincidences in life and you are all acquainted with the basic philosophy of doing good for others and the earth while you are in physical manifestation. You all made the commitment, before you came back into physical form on the earth plane, to assist all during this time of transition. Whatever your current role, know that you have impacted others and continue to impact others with your energy. Therefore, it is important to focus on reality, as you see it.

Your reality is what is true for you and each of you look at your lives from different realities. This doesn't mean that you can't accomplish great things in concert with one another; it just means that everyone approaches things from their own perspective. I am here to tell you that it is important that you tune inside to awaken to that which will help you meet your commitment.

I offer my help in this adventure. I can help you create miracles and give you courage to accept the miracles in your life. I offer you help with courage, protection and direction in your life. If you find yourself in a quandary, just say my name and I will arrive to provide you with creative ideas for solving the quandary. It is important for you to understand that you are all light-workers. You all carry vibrations, which enable you to reach beyond the mundane quagmires that some of you find yourselves enmeshed in. You are all vibrating at a rate that allows you to know things faster than most.

You will all find, at times, that you know things and have no idea how you know. It is because of who you are. Have no fear of these gifts. Now is the time for you to awaken to these gifts and to begin to use them. Learn to trust that information, which seems to come from nowhere; it is merely you awakening to the connection you have with Spirit and the universal wisdom. I tell you, that you can perform miracles and you have the right to step into who you are without fear or doubt about your abilities. Now is the time! You are needed in all capacities. Open your hearts and your eyes to the signs which are all around you, confirming that you are light-workers! When you awaken to the connection, when you allow yourself to believe that you are connected to the all and can manifest miracles in your life, then you will know serenity and peace. Then you will live with confidence, because you will know that you don't need to control or prove yourself to anyone. You will feel the strength of this connection and know the power which is within you.

I leave you with this thought: You are all light-workers and now is the time to acknowledge this in your hearts, because the sooner you acknowledge this, the sooner you will live your life according to your highest good. I will come to help you stand in courage and strength, with protection and love, just call my name.

I thank you for reading this and send you much love, protection and courage as you move into a new space, both in your mind and in your life.

Twenty-Eight

Mother Mary

I come today to bring you love. My only purpose for today is to engulf you with unconditional love. You are all my children and I love you and will protect you with all my heart. Love is the balm of healing. I send you healing through the love that is yours just for being. Sit with open hearts and trust that you deserve this love; feel it in your very cells, filling you and surrounding you.

I see each of you struggle daily to live up to your own expectations and I say to you, "Love yourselves, as I love you!" Have compassion for yourselves and all that you are, as I do. Take the time to just sit in my love and know that I am holding you in my heart and in my arms, as a mother holds her child; sharing with you all the love and protection you deserve. I share this love with you and ask that you accept it with joy; I ask nothing of you, except that you be willing to receive the love and joy I offer.

As you go through your day, just call my name and I will surround you and fill you with my love. Let this love bring joy and laughter into your life, as these are healing for you, emotionally, physically and mentally. When you call on me, know that I am here for you, offering my support and encouraging you to be all that you are. I encourage you to live your life to the fullest, with lots of joy and laughter. Accept my love and go forth, knowing that I am here to provide support and encouragement in everything you do. Know that you are free to return to me for whatever support you need. Whenever you find yourself in need of being held as a mother would hold you, call on me and envision yourself being held, cuddled and protected in my arms, as you were held in your own mother's arms.

I am here for you! I thank you for reading my message and accepting the love and protection I give to you. Surround and fill yourself with this all- encompassing love and let it lead you to a joyful day.

Twenty-Nine

St. John of God

I come to you today to help you move above your problems and concerns. Give your concerns to God and trust that everything will be good. I find it important to share with you the gift of laughter, as it will help to disperse depression and anxiety. When you find that you are stuck and feeling anxious or depressed, you can call on me to help you change your focus.

Laughter can help to get you above the problems you feel plague your life. I will assist you in releasing your concerns and issues, to Spirit. By turning you cares and concerns over, you then can release your need to control. The need to control comes from your fear that you are alone and unable to trust that you are safe. I am here to tell you to trust that you are always connected.

When you release your need to control and focus your thoughts on lighter things, you allow information to come into your hearts and minds, which will bring the solution to that which concerns you. Be open to the idea that laughter can help clear many things up. Be open to the idea that laughter and joy can help in finding a solution.

As you know, when you change your focus, you can change

the feelings which are contributing to depression and anxiety. As those of you in the earth plane say, "Laughter can be the best medicine." Laughter is something that can be used to release feelings of tension, fear and doubt. It can help to put things into perspective, so that you may step back and understand what is happening from a distance, rather than staying stuck in the muck.

Call on me and I will help, or at least remind you, that you don't always have to be in charge to ensure that things will work out to your satisfaction. You are loved and we care. Call on me or any of your other angels, spirit guides or ascended masters. We await your call and have the desire to serve.

Thank you for reading this message and I send you laughter, light and love to assist you in this day.

Thirty

Maitreya

As you can tell by my other name, I come today to talk to you about how laughter and music lead to enlightenment. I look upon all of you, striving daily in everything you do and then, along with the striving, you add worry and fear. I tell you, the striving, worry and fear combine within you to close you off to that which is waiting to manifest in your life. I do not say that you should sit and do nothing, but that what you do could be done with lightness and laughter in your heart and with less stress.

Give your worry, fear and concern to me. I can change things and help you look at life with a lighter eye. The more you close yourself off, the less you will be able to see and know that opportunities are just in front of you. Laughter and music open your hearts and energy, the very breath that you release through laughter also releases constricted energy within you. This then opens you up to be able to accept, with an open heart and mind, that which is awaiting your acknowledgment.

Laughter and music are the very breath of life. When you can laugh at things, they don't seem so difficult or over-whelming. Laughter can assist you in refocusing your thoughts, if only for a short time. I say to you, laughter and music are as important in your life as striving and constantly reaching for success! In fact, I say to you that laughter and music are even more important. Let yourself breathe, let yourself laugh and feel the release and the weight being lifted. Sing, laugh and enjoy the present, as you can't change the past and you don't know what the future may bring.

I thank you for reading and send you lightness and laughter, asking only that you release your concerns and worries to me. I can help! Join me in singing and laughing every day.

Thirty-One

Ashtar

I am from another dimension and for most of you my appearance is subtle, because most of you are defined by three dimensions and are not aware of the greater connection with all of the cosmos. I have come today to let you know that you are supported during all of the changes, which are taking place on your earth. I will help you be protected and I will help you release the fears you have about the many changes, which are taking place in the earth plane today.

As most of you know, the vibratory rate is increasing and therefore, much of what you have known to be true is in a state of flux. You have chosen to be here during this time to assist with the changes. Many of you feel that you need assistance with these changes as well, but I say to you, "Go within and yet expand your awareness beyond the three dimensions and you will have a greater understanding of the changes."

You may call on me for protection during this time and I will help you release the fears that keep you framed within a limited time, space dimension. The more that you can be open to the unlimited time and space, the more comfortable you will be here and now.

You are all here as guides, to assist those who have not yet awakened to the Divine within. Do not be afraid, for what you become more aware of is the shift from fear and darkness to peace and understanding. This does not mean that things will always change smoothly, but you can help when you keep your focus on the light. Acknowledge that which you judge to be dark and troubling, but know that you are the master of your own reality and once you have brought the troubles into the light, then you can release them, as in a puff of smoke.

Those of us from other dimensions are here to assist you with the changes and help you to evolve toward your highest self. I come as an emissary of those others from dimensions beyond those with which you are familiar. We honor you for choosing this time to incarnate on the earth plane. Open your mind and call on me for help or to answer questions about places beyond.

I send you love, light, and assistance as you move into your highest self.

Thirty-Two

Archangel Raziel

I come to you today to offer you my services in unlocking the esoteric information of the universe. You all have the ability to access this information; you just don't trust the information when you receive it, because you believe that you are not worthy to know this. I tell you that you are all divine and as such you have access to the all. I can help you!

You are all capable of sharing the information with others and now is the time for you to listen and step forth with this knowledge. Just call on me and I will assist you to open your eyes and hearts to that which can help you and others, on the earth plane, to live your lives from the highest.

Many of you doubt that you can access this knowledge and you believe that this is what holds you back from fully realizing your power. I say to you, "Fear and belief that you are unworthy is what holds you back!" Now is the time to bring your beliefs up into the light, so that you can release them and begin to receive all that is yours for the asking. This, too, is one of the secrets of manifesting.

You work hard to manifest things into your life and some of you succeed to a limited degree. I say to you, "Where you set your limits is far lower than what you are capable of receiving!"

Look into yourselves and check your beliefs about your life. Look into how you feel about receiving everything you ask for. Is this a frightening thought and do you doubt that you are truly able to manifest that which you desire? I am here to tell you that most of you need to look at your beliefs and release those which do not serve you. Know that the more you can manifest into your life the more you can help others along their path. Stop limiting yourselves based on old programming and old beliefs.

Many of you come from cultures that have led you to believe that you are sinners and therefore, must either work very hard or never receive anything above that which your society and your family feel you deserve. Know that this is a belief that holds you back! Be willing to release this belief and all other beliefs, which you carry from your upbringing or from past lives. This is here and now and I tell you that you are divine and worthy of all knowledge, all love, all prosperity and everything your heart desires! Do not fear that if you receive, then others will have to lose. This is another belief that you need to release!

Be willing to look at your beliefs and change and release them. Once you have done this you will be amazed at what you can generate in your life and how much more you will be able to share with those around you.

You are all worthy of more than you allow yourself to receive. Now is the time to change! Now is the time to accept the gifts that are offered. Open your hearts and minds to release those old beliefs and receive all that you desire.

I send you assistance to release your old beliefs and help

you move into the knowledge and belief that you are worthy. May love, prosperity and your connection to the universe be the path you choose.

Thirty-Three

Kuan Ti

I come today to talk to you about leadership and what you, as spiritual beings on the earth plane, can do as you move further into the 21st century. It is important for you to look inside yourselves and know what you want in a leader.

I am called a warrior, because when I lived on the earth plane I was a warrior, but one who eventually chose understanding and acceptance of differences rather than fear and control, which causes war and strife.

What kind of leader do you want? What kind of leader are you? It is time for all to go into the innermost recesses of your soul and ask, "What can I do now to bring peace to myself and those around me?" It begins with you!

The more often you operate from fear and control, the more it propagates that behavior in others. Fear is very powerful and the more fearful you are, the more control you wish to have. When you come from a place of understanding and compassion, both for yourselves and others, then you can work with others to reach a mutually supportive decision. The more you accept yourself and everything about you, the less you rely on the approval of others. This, therefore, opens you up to the idea that you don't always have to be right and not everyone has to agree with you. This, in turn, allows others to express themselves and hopefully begin to accept that they are perfect just the way they are, with their own opinions and ideas. Fear and control block this experience from all concerned.

Fear and control, whether it exists in a family, business or government is meant to stifle self-expression and creativity. Think about where you are in this. Where do you operate? Are you fearful, and if so, how can you release the fear, so that you can empower yourself and others to be the most creative, open, caring people they can be?

I will help you release your fears and need to control. Call on me when you question how your behavior is affecting you. The more you come from understanding, the more at peace you will be within yourself and the more power you will have to live your life from the highest place. This will open your heart and your life to unexpected blessings.

So I leave you with this: Release your fears and your need to control will be released as well. Look to your leaders and ask for assistance in helping them release their fears, so the need for control will disappear and everyone will begin to support one another to be the best that they can be. I give you my support as you work toward this goal.

I send you blessings and wisdom as you walk this path, realizing that we are all connected and the more we help one another, the more we learn and grow in the most positive ways.

Thirty-Four

Moses

I come today to talk about leadership. It is time for you to know that all who receive this message are leaders. I can see some of you have doubt about this and I am here to assure you that it is true. You have all committed to this role. This was done prior to your incarnation into this life. You will be leaders in a variety of ways and now is the time to step into that role!

If you are unsure about how you will lead, spend some time connecting with Spirit. I can hear you saying you have tried and you still don't know what you are to do. I say to you, "Spend time going within and listening to the answers!" Some of you will not believe how you are to lead and will throw doubt into your mind. This is not the way to listen. Open your minds and hearts to the message!

The more questions you ask, the more answers will come to you. Listen for the answers and if what you are hearing doesn't make sense, ask for clarification. You have the right to not only ask for clarification, but in your conversation with Spirit, ask for some direction in the way you are to step up to your leadership role. You have direct communication with Spirit.

You do not need any intermediary!

Understand that what you hear inside, which seems to come from someone else, actually is one of the ways that you are communicating with Spirit and Spirit is talking to you.

Another way that information can be passed on to you is if you ask for a physical sign. These signs can be found on advertising or vehicles. Be aware that there are many ways this information can be communicated.

Do not doubt that you have come into the earth plane this time to be a leader. Trust that the way will open before you when you begin to trust, that every time you have been placed in a leadership position, regardless of how small, you are being prepared to step into a bigger role. Take a look at your life; look for times when you have had to take the lead. Look at what you did and how it happened and know that this was not a mistake. Be aware, that your abilities are consistent with leadership. You have much to teach and now is the time to come forth. Do not hold back, because of fear. Do not hold back, because you doubt you are qualified. Trust that you have all the tools and abilities you need to be in the position. I will help you move into this position, as I, too, felt doubt, but did it anyway.

I leave you with this thought: The world needs you now! You have, within you, all that you will need and others see you as a leader, even if you don't. Be a beacon for others to step into their power and abilities!

I thank you for reading this message and send blessings, love and support on your path.

Thirty-Five

Dana

I come today to talk to you about releasing the illusion that you are less than you are. I am here to tell you that I am honored to serve you. It is apparent that most of you fail to see the glory of you.

You are all royalty and I place a crown and royal robes upon your person. Sit with this and know that you deserve to wear these. Feel the wealth and abundance when you allow yourself to realize that this is your position by divine right.

As you know, you are all connected to one another and to the greater universe. You are all Spirit made manifest and as such, you have gifts and abilities, which you attribute to the Divine. You are capable of great things and now is the time to do what you are here to do. You are capable of divine magic and creation.

I come before you to offer my services in supporting your efforts to reach your potential. As has been discussed by others, you are leaders, but you can't lead effectively if you can't accept who you are, even though you find yourself in leadership roles through no effort on your part. You do know that people turn to you for advice and help. Accept this and know that you are trusted to provide assistance and leadership in many situations. You say, "Who am I?" You say, "I am not worthy!" You say, "I am not qualified!" I say to all of you about these ideas, "Release them and step into your rightful place! Give these feelings to God!"

Know that somewhere, in your heart, you are aware of your nature and can accept it. Now is the time to go inside and allow the greatness, which is you, to shine forth! You can lean on me if you feel uncomfortable with this.

Do not feel that you have to take a giant step in this direction. I say to you, "Just take one step." One small step will begin your journey and help you achieve that for which you came into this life. One small step leads to another and then another. Take a cloth and wipe a small corner in the window of your soul center and allow just a small amount of light to shine forth. Do not be afraid! All of us in the other realms support you and the work you are doing. Honor yourself for what you bring to this life. Erase the illusion that you are less than.

You all come with your own unique gifts and it is time to release any illusions that you lack the tools and gifts that are necessary to provide you with everything you need in this time and place. It is important for all that you release the self-deception that you are not worthy! Know that you are greater than you can imagine, and do not allow your mind to confuse you with its constant chatter about old rules and regulations. It is time to get beyond the mind to your higher self and your connection with the universal wisdom. Take your place in the greater scheme of things. Let yourself fly free, without doubt and fear. Acknowledge the divine being you are, and the leadership skills you possess will surface to provide assistance for yourselves and others in magnificent ways.

I thank you for reading this message and say, "I am honored to serve you!" Take the time today to sit and visualize yourself, enfolded in a royal robe with a crown on your head. See it, feel it and then allow this to sink into every cell in your body. I send blessings, great love and all the support.

Thirty-Six

Melchizedek

⚬~⚬

I come today to speak of esoteric knowledge and healing. You all have the ability to know, that which you are not sure how you know. There is much information that is hidden from the mass consciousness, but that is accessible by opening your connection to the Divine.

I come to tell you that it is time for you to study that which comes from within, when your hearts and minds are open. Do not always look outside of yourselves for information and study. Now is the time to quiet your minds and allow information to come to you from the universal wisdom. You all have the ability to access this information. Call on me and I can help you unlock the door to this information

This information is important to you and the earth plane at this time. Prepare yourselves to gain much by sitting and listening. There is much to be taught, but you must still your busy minds and listen to that which comes from your connection with the Divine. These tools are given to assist you along your path. This information will benefit you during the shifts and changes which are taking place in your world. Now is the time to awaken to this form of study and wisdom, as it is needed now. Know that the information you receive is truth! You can tap into it when you are willing. Be willing now! Call on me to assist you in this venture.

I can help quiet your mind and open your cells and heart to the esoteric information, which is not in any book, but only in the great wisdom of all. Trust your knowing and if you doubt, then ask that only information which is derived from the light be allowed to enter your being.

I can help release doubts and fears about this, as well as help you to look at what could be termed dark energies with understanding. Know that I will assist only if you use this esoteric information in a positive way. Should you choose to use the information to do harm, you will not receive my help.

Now is the time to take another step along the path. I tell you, "There is much to learn and much to absorb, so open your hearts and still your minds and be prepared to learn." You are all very powerful and this will assist you in using your power in the most effective manner.

I thank you for listening and send you blessings, love and divine magic.

Thirty-Seven

Saint Germain

Today I come to give you courage to be who you are; to let you know that you are in the right place at the right time. You have all chosen this time to be here. You are all leaders among others, and I am here to help you know and understand your role. Release your fears and everything which is blocking you from stepping into your divine purpose. I am here for you to assist in this process.

I can see that you have many pressures in your lives, but are they real or are they something that the mind sets up and enforces to keep you stuck?

You are more than your mind! You are much greater than your physical, mental and emotional self. You are Divine and as such, you have the capabilities to release yourself from the beliefs and fears, which keep you stuck. I can hear you saying, "I'm trying to release all of this." I say, "Don't try, just do it!" What I mean is to be willing to release everything that prevents you from being your true self here and now. You can do it! We all support you in this.

Open your hearts to joy and laughter. Open your hearts to the world and beyond. I will be there as will many others, as you release these things that hold you back. Do not fear change, as it is happening always, with or without your knowledge and permission.

Now step into your passion. Open up to the glorious things that you can manifest here and now. Go forth without fear knowing that you are taking your rightful place in the world and as you do, you will be giving to the greater good. You are just at the edge of it. Do not let fear which is groundless, keep you stuck!

Your cares and concerns are real in your mind. Release them to me and to others of the higher realms and we will support you. The only caution is to take these steps with the anticipation of a child.

Look to the changes as joyful and light, for if you think this is hard work then it only prevents you from accepting the grace that is yours. I thank you for reading and leave you with this thought: We are all here to support you and wish to help you even command information and healing. I send blessings, joy, laughter and light. Sing your way through your day today.

Thirty-Eight

Lu-Hsing

Today, I wish to discuss one way to success and financial abundance in whatever you do. I say to you, "You must maintain a warrior attitude about your relationships in the business world and in your quest for abundance." By this, I mean you must persevere and not quit right before the windfall arrives. Do not give up hope, but expect a positive outcome for everything. It also means being flexible, while working toward your goal. The more flexible you are, the more you will have the ability to move in directions that you need to with short thought.

Warriors expect positive outcomes when they engage. When you are prepared and flexible along with maintaining a positive attitude, you will be in a better position to succeed. I will assist you as you work toward your goals. Be aware that my approach is subtle and, therefore, when you call on me you must listen closely, but know that I will be here to assist!

Another aspect of being a warrior is to work from a position of diplomacy and trust. You must be able to make pacts with yourself and others that you can keep. If you know that you can trust yourself to follow through with what you have agreed to, then you can trust that you will be true to yourself in all ways.

Perseverance the ability to be diplomatic the ability to make agreements and keep them, expecting positive outcomes and trust are all the things that will bring abundance and success in the world and in life. Know that all of these skills are within. Know that you are capable of all of these things and that with these attitudes and actions you are on the path.

Whenever you are in a negotiation or in a big meeting, you may call on me to assist you. I will be there to help smooth the way, so the outcome will be for the highest good of all concerned.

Today you step forward with a positive outlook and a persevering attitude. I thank you for reading this and send you good fortune and many blessings.

Thirty-Nine

Artemis

I come to you today to talk about connecting with the divine feminine and the power within. You all have the divine feminine within, whether you are male or female. I am here to assist you in connecting with it.

Learn to trust your intuition, as it is one of the ways that you get information from the universal wisdom. Many say that women are more intuitive than men. This in some ways is true, because women have used their intuition throughout their lives, whereas men do not acknowledge it; they, instead, refer to it as a gut reaction.

Your intuition can be of great assistance in your life. It is a precursor to a deeper connection with Spirit. The more you open yourself to the connection with your intuition, the more information you will get from Spirit.

All of you get information from your intuition, but a lot of you reject it or ignore it, because the information doesn't always agree with what your other senses are telling you. The information you are getting from your intuition is deeper and comes from a wider source. Start to use it more, start to open to it and when you follow your intuition see what happens!

Allow yourself to ask a question and then listen for the answer and follow what you are told to do. Start with a drive and ask where you should turn or which route you should take. Trust that there is a reason you are being directed from within to do something specific. You will find that you can count on your intuition to lead you to things for your highest good. Start small and soon you will find that you can trust it in bigger situations.

As you use your intuition you will find a greater connection with the feminine within. You will learn that the divine feminine is highly creative and far thinking.

Many of you work primarily with your left brain and function in a linear way. Now is the time to look at what your right brain can bring to solving problems. The feminine within can assist in finding solutions to problems in your life from a creative perspective rather than a linear one. Use your feminine energy to open you up to a wider way of looking at life.

You are all awakening and now is the time to use all that is within you to heal yourself and to open to the joy, laughter and peace that awaits you, as you open to the greatness that is within.

I send you love, light, laughter and joy. Call on me to assist with trusting your intuition and the divine feminine within.

Forty

Ida-Ten

∽

I come today to offer you my support with regard to your spirituality. All of you come from various spiritual backgrounds and many of you are moving into spiritual philosophies that are different from those with which you were raised. I offer you my support and help in preventing ridicule from others when you speak of your new ideas and beliefs. I will protect you from ridicule. Understand that people use ridicule and hostility when they don't understand things.

Many people are afraid of what they don't understand and rather than open up to new information, they choose to become sarcastic and disdainful. Often, they will imply that you are dim-witted and dull if you have faith and spiritual beliefs. I tell you, "It doesn't matter what others think about this!" It is important to you what your beliefs are. It is important to you and only you how you chose to live your life! Your relationship with Spirit is between you and Spirit, so remember that you don't have to answer to anyone other than yourself in this regard.

I am here to assist you in being comfortable expressing your beliefs without fear. You have a right to your beliefs and philosophy, as long as it harms no one. Know that your spiritual practices are practices that you do to enrich your life and to solidify your connection to Spirit.

Whenever you feel that you are being criticized, call on me and I will help smooth the way. It is important to keep in mind that what you do for you is up to you! You make the choices which affect your life. You do the practices which help you connect and are healing for your soul. You are the most important person in your life and only you can decide how you want to live your life and whether Spirit is going to play an active role in it.

Your spiritual beliefs can smooth the way for you in this life on the earth plane, so do not let others influence how you believe and what you do to foster that belief. You are each individuals and you each hold unique beliefs, don't be afraid that you are wrong. What is appropriate for one is not necessarily appropriate for another.

Be also aware that you can't force your beliefs and philosophy on another. You must feel free to discuss your spiritual beliefs, but do not have expectations that everyone must have the same beliefs. Be open to others and have your discussions, but understand that you each have the right to your own beliefs.

Call on me when you find yourself being ridiculed for your beliefs and I will help you. I send you blessings, love and protection in all that you do.

Forty-One

Brigit

With great respect, I come to you today to honor you, you of great strength and understanding, you of great power and gentleness, you who have awakened to the spirit within! I am here to stand beside you and help you, as you move further into your awakening and as you speak to others about what you know.

We of the other realms are all available to help you acknowledge your gifts and use them for the highest good of all. We see you begin to slowly take the steps that open you to the all that is yours by divine right and we support and applaud your efforts.

We know that some of you are taking tentative steps and that you hold fear and doubt about your gifts and the role you are to play in this life. Call on me when you are unsure about the information you receive after asking your guides and angels what is your next step or your role today. I will help you release the doubt about your abilities and your fear of being to open with the information you possess.

You may call on me to release the fear and the doubt that comes upon you when you decide to follow your guidance from within. Each of you has awakened to that which is within and each of you faces your own illusions, that you are not worthy and that there is some mistake on the part of Spirit. I tell you that there is no mistake and you are worthy of things that, to you, are amazing and to us are merely examples of using your gifts for the highest good of all.

Do not fear that you are speaking of things that are beyond your ability to know. You have within you the connection with the universal wisdom and you already know more than you know you know. It is time for each of you to release the beliefs that you are unworthy and unqualified. Listen to that which comes from within and know that whenever the information is of a positive nature and is leading you closer to Spirit, that this information is correct.

Call on me to assist you in releasing these fears and to help with your strength to be who you are here and now, today. I will stand beside you and support you as you move more fully into your divine purpose. You are perfect beyond your wildest imagination and you are capable of knowing and doing many things beyond anything you currently understand.

All of us from the other realms are waiting for you to call on us to help make your life easier and to ensure that you will feel supported and joyful as you take your rightful place among the teachers and mystics on the earth plane today.

I thank you for reading this and repeat, "Call on us whenever you wish confirmation or information about your choices." We can also go before you to sweep the path you walk, so that it is less of a struggle. I give you great respect and love and I welcome you into your awakening self.

Forty-Two

Archangel Sandalphon

I come today to talk to you about music; it is everywhere! Listen to the music in nature and it can change your heart. Hear the birds sing, the leaves rustle, the water flow in the creek or river and with each sound, open your heart to the love that is being sent to you from Spirit.

Music is all around you every day; at times, it is a cacophony with many discordant notes all coming together, to create noise and at other times, it is an orchestra sending notes that soar or dance; both will influence how you approach your day.

Listen to what is around you today! What type of music are you playing in your mind, in your heart, in your physical world? The music that you surround yourself with can influence your life. It is your choice, but be aware that it does affect you in every facet of your being.

Try an experiment: the next time you are feeling upset, surround yourself with music that soars to the heavens, that brings laughter to your heart and joy to your ears. See how long you remain in the doldrums.

Music is a wonder that all can share and enjoy. I say to you, "Make good use of the music that is in your life to assist you in expressing what you are thinking and feeling and also to change the way you are thinking and feeling!" Music permeates the very cells in you. Music fills you and surrounds you every day of your life, as it is the sounds of people chattering, the sounds of a busy city and the sounds of the country. Open your hearts and your ears and listen to what it is telling you.

Music can help you manifest your desires. Play, hum or sing while you are thinking about that which you desire. Music will enhance your ability to manifest; that is why chanting is so powerful in helping you to awaken to your connection to Spirit.

I bring this to you today to help you celebrate your day. To live in the moment with joy and awareness of the wonderment that surrounds you. Listen to the music of your heart and the earth as they speak to you of love, light, joy and laughter; then send it out into the world to bring these feelings to all.

You are all grand musicians playing music on an instrument or with your voice. Let the music fill the world to assist all and bring everything to a higher vibration.

I thank you for reading this message and leave you with this thought: You can live a life filled with music that thrills your heart or you can live it with music that creates tension and heartache. This is your choice!

I send you music that thrills and delights you, awakening you to your divine self. Live today surrounded by music that brings joy, light and laughter and walk into the world sharing this positive energy with everyone you meet.

Forty-Three

Sanat Kumara

I come to you to speak of power. You are all powerful. Do not fear the word power, for it doesn't relate to power over anyone or anything but you. It has more to do with your ability to stand up for your beliefs in the face of ridicule and criticism. It has to do with living your life without fear and doubt. It is about living authentically from within and following that which you know to be true and joyful.

The power of which I speak is a power which involves living joyously and fully in the true spirit of you. It is that which allows you to be fully and completely giving and loving without fear. Power allows you to engage in discussions without having to win. It is flexible and open to other points of view, because you are strong within yourself.

Now is the time to take back your power! Now is the time to take a stand and let yourself know that you are worthy of everything the universe has to offer and you are powerful enough to share it and not operate from a place of lack. Now is the time to acknowledge the power within you and to enfold yourself with this knowledge and the peace that it brings. Now is the time to take control of your life and your beliefs and discard those beliefs which do not support you in your living from your highest most powerful place, of love and understanding. Now is the time!

You are needed now, with your full strength and power, to assist in the process which is happening throughout the earth plane and beyond. You are very powerful and it is time that you awaken to the power that is within you to heal, to manifest, to love, to bring peace, to bring joy and laughter and light. Allow the powerful light, which is within, to shine forth and accept that this power that is already inside of you is now ready to be used for the highest good of all. Accept that You are powerful! Accept that This is your birthright! Accept that this is a power that is needed at this time and that it is loving and flowing from you, even though you may try to deny it!

If this power that is inside of you is uncomfortable for you to accept or to understand, lean on me and I will support you and show you the way. Call on me and I will be there for you! You will feel my strength and the power that resides in me, as I share and connect with you. Know that I can assist you in attracting only the highest energies. I will provide a loving, safe environment for you to grow into, accepting and acknowledging the power you possess.

Do not be afraid as this is the power of Spirit that resides in you and it is creative and loving, rather than destructive and controlling. This power gives you and others the freedom to be. It is a force that goes beyond that which you know at this time.

Awaken to the power within, feel the freedom and lightness that exists when you are in your power. I repeat, "YOU ARE POWERFUL!"

I send you love, strength and assistance in awakening to your power. Live in it, love in it and be free.

Forty-Four

Archangel Gabriel

I come before you today to offer my support as you step forward and into your divine power and light. All of you are a gift to the earth plane at this time.

This, as many of you know, is a time of transition and the energies are shifting from density to light. Each of you brings your own light to this process and you add your ability to empower others in lightness to the shift. I come to encourage you all to become more than you have been. Now is the time for you to bring your powerful light up and out, shining on the earth as a beacon of hope and healing. You are all needed NOW!

Those of us in the other realms see your doubt and your fear. We support all that you are and all that you came here to do. Now is the time for you to realize your powerful light and wisdom and to share it with the world around you!

If you are unsure what to do, call on us and go inside! Listen for the answer! You can request a more physical answer to the question and the answer will appear in a more physical way. Choose whichever way suits you, but please stop procrastinating, as you are needed now!

It is important to understand that you have wisdom to share with others, be it on a one to one basis or in groups. Be open to whichever way this chooses to manifest in your life. Call on us to ease the way for this manifestation. We will come to lend you strength and support.

I can help pave the way for you to be more fully present to those who need you. I can open doors, so that the messages you are here to provide can be given to the largest number of people in the shortest period of time. I can help you release your fear and doubt and open your hearts, so that the wisdom you impart is of the highest.

Know that the information you need is already within you and that all you have to do is allow it to come forth. Know that when you wish to communicate with others you can impact them on many levels, in ways that can empower them to also be whom they are meant to be at this time and place.

I come to inform and encourage you to shine your light upon the earth every minute of every day; send it out around you and speak with the power that is within you. I am here to acknowledge and honor the greatness that is within each and every one of you. It is with great respect that I tell you that you are more powerful than you realize and wiser than you know!

Allow this power and wisdom to come forth from you and help to make the earth plane a brighter, more peaceful place with acceptance and understanding of all points of view.

Speak your truth, yet accept that what is your truth is not always someone else's truth. What is important for you to remember is that when you speak your truth, you help to open the hearts of others and give them the opportunity to look at things in a different way.

With great respect and honor I tell you, now is the time to open your hearts and be the bright, loving, glorious beings you are! Now is the time to spread your light, love and wisdom in the earth!

We are here to support your efforts and guide your way.

Forty-Five

Archangel Uriel

⌒◡◡)

My name means "Light of God" and I come today to talk about you accessing your own light. Your light is within and without, it fills you and surrounds you at all times. Some of you wander around with your light shrouded in darkness. This is to say that you wish to keep your light hidden for whatever reason. Know that your light will shine, regardless of what you do to hide it!

Some of you hide out, thinking that your light is not necessary or is unimportant. Some of you doubt that you even have a light. I am here to tell you that you are all filled with light, although some of your lights are operating at what could be termed low wattage, which sends out very little. It is time for you to polish that which surrounds your light and allow your light to shine brightly into the world!

The more your light shines, the less that can be hidden. It is as if you bring light into a darkened room. One light brings much that was hidden into clarity.

It is now time for the light to bring into the open many esoteric things that have been used to control people. The ability to control people must be released! The more information that can be brought into the light, the more your decisions can come from a place of knowledge and understanding.

Things that are in the dark and hidden can create chaos and fear, because they cannot be known or understood. The more that these things are brought into the light, the lower the fear and anxiety will be. Your light will assist others to allow their light to shine, without fear of repercussions from those who don't understand the light.

When you are unsure about your light, call on me to assist you. I will help you turn up the light from within. Your light is glorious and is needed now!

Know that you are powerful, light filled beings and that your purpose on the earth plane is to live your life from the light that is within, so that others may be free to do the same. You are powerful and your powerful light can be a beacon to those who live in fear and doubt. Trust that you are the light and that you can use this light to access information to assist you on your path. Turn to your light for information, understanding and healing. Live your life from a light-filled place and with a joyful, open heart.

Know that you are being guided and protected as you share your light. Call on us for assistance and we will be there!

I send you light, love, joy and blessings as you go through your day. Share all that you are every day and watch your world change.

Forty-Six

Maat

Truth and integrity are important in today's world. I come to you today to offer my help in discerning truth in others and, when you call on me, even in yourself.

You have the ability, within you, to find the truth of a situation or of people, but often you don't trust what you are intuitively receiving. It is time for you to trust that information, as it will aid you in your quest for the better world. You are all gifted with the ability to gain information and insight, by turning within and trusting that which you receive. I will assist you in this effort.

Your truth will help you to open your hearts and your minds to the light that is within and to the greater world. When you operate from truth, you live your life in integrity and from the highest place. This will bring peace and harmony into your life. Your ability to know what you hear or see as truth will also assist in your pursuit of healing and understanding.

Know that not everyone who speaks of Spirit comes from Spirit. Not everyone who tells you of the new way of doing things, or suggests that you need to study this or that to enhance your spiritual or creative abilities, is coming from truth. It is important, therefore, that you trust what your heart or as some of you say, "your gut" is telling you.

Some, who are out there speaking of new ways and new thinking, are only seeking fame and fortune. Some are looking to gather followers and instead of empowering you, will pull you in and have you serve them instead of yourself, as they are into obtaining power over others. Trust what you know! Trust what you are feeling about any situation if it is in your best interest. Remember, the more you trust yourself and love yourself, the more you can give to others.

Do not believe everything you read or hear! Listen to the truth that lies within you. Whenever you are in doubt about someone, call on me and I will help you know the truth. Understand that I come from truth, so if you do not want to know this, do not call on me!

I tell you to listen to your inner voice and trust that you are being led toward your highest good. Whenever you are unsure about whether to take a class or seminar or to believe what you read, turn within and if you don't trust what you feel or hear, then call on me and I will assist you. I will help you know the truth and I will assist you in learning to trust what you know. Truth and integrity will lead you to your highest good.

I send you blessings and love. Know that I await your call to assist you in knowing the truth about any given situation. Be at peace and trust that which you already know.

Forty-Seven

Maitreya

I am often referred to as the "Laughing Buddha" and I come today to share my delight in you and the progress you are making in your lives. You are all expanding and opening to the glory that is you. I know some of you wish that this could happen immediately, but to know that it is happening is enough for now!

Many of you look at this as work. You see change as frightening and yet move toward it anyway and I applaud you for walking through your fear!

Now is the time to be gentle with yourself. Lighten up and approach your development with an open heart filled with light, laughter and love. Accept that you are doing all you can from a work point of view. Now is the time to let things develop at their own pace, without pushing to move forward.

You are all beautiful and it is time for you to acknowledge this and to live more fully in the present. Your striving has accomplished much, but now it is time to enjoy the fruits of your labor and know that as you sing, dance and laugh you are also connecting with Spirit and all that is.

It is true music, laughter and joy can help you connect with your highest self and Spirit. It is time to laugh and not take yourself and your life so seriously. When you laugh and sing even, in the midst of sorrow, you lighten your load; life becomes easier and your connection to Spirit, greater!

It helps if you can look at your life as a play and you are writing the script. How do you wish to write the current act, as a comedy or tragedy? It is your choice! Even if it is a tragedy, can you approach it with gusto? I see many of you becoming totally involved in the tragic acts, but failing to approach the comedy. Create some comedy and lighten your heart!

Look at where you are right this moment and see if you can feel that you have gratitude and even a small thing to smile about. Look around you at the glorious earth and share a smile, just for being in it here and now. Your spring is in the air and all of the beautiful earth is beginning to bloom; approach it with a smile and watch yourself bloom as well!

Today is the day you sing, dance and laugh! Today is the day you live, even if for a moment, in the energy and light of laughter. Call on me and I will assist you! It is a joy to me to be able to help you bring joy and laughter into your life; to lighten your load and help you to realize that all your work is successful and you are on your way to more joy than you have known.

You need to open your hearts to the joy that is present in your life right now. Do not wait to laugh, sing and dance. Celebrate you now! Be grateful to yourself now! Set aside today and smile, laugh and sing for at least a short time, and see what happens. Call on me to help you grow, through joy and laughter, rather than pain. As you laugh, you breathe in the all and you release that which doesn't serve you.

I send you laughter, light and joy to fill your day and offer my assistance as you continue growing through joy, rather than pain. Try it, just for today.

Forty-Eight

Archangel Haniel

I come to you today to encourage you to connect with the light and energy of the moon. The moon is filled with powerful light and energy, which will help you in healing and connecting more closely with the divine feminine.

If you are involved in working with herbs and potions, call on me to help you increase your connection to the moon and its healing light. The moon is powerful and affects all, as evidenced by the tide of the ocean and other bodies of water. Your moon connection will also assist you in opening yourself to clairvoyance and other sight.

I encourage you to touch the moon energy within you. Notice that when the moon is full, people and animals take on different ways of being. Do not fear this, but listen to what happens to you when you are more connected with the moon. It is amazing what happens when you allow the moon to become a greater part of your life. The energy and light from the moon create a greater, more open connection with the power of the divine feminine.

You are all powerful and you all contain aspects of the divine feminine. Now you are being called to this power which resides within you. This is a power which approaches life in a gentle manner; this moves you to stand in your power of self. The divine feminine is slowly becoming more prevalent in your world. Know that you will notice a strong presence of the feminine coming to the fore. Now is the time!

You have all lived with the warrior who is aggressive, fierce and war-like. Now is the time of the warrior who can work toward understanding and acceptance. This warrior is no less fierce than the previous warrior, but the energy comes from a different place, a place filled with the desire and ability to work together for a better world for all.

I come today to offer my support as you move into this new energy and light. It is time! I have observed the work you have all done, moving yourselves toward this energy and I say to you that you are not alone. I say that for every act of terror and war, there are innumerable acts of kindness and sharing, whether on a one-to-one basis or in groups.

I see you moving in a direction of caring and sharing. When you come from your power, when you allow the divine feminine to share with the divine masculine on an equal basis within, you then have balance. Once the balance is achieved, you no longer need to fight to be right. As you move into a position where you accept that it is OK for each to have their own beliefs and opinions, you move into a more peaceful existence.

Be gentle with yourself, you have worked hard to change! Know that your hard work is impressive from my perspective. Know that I see all of you becoming more of what you committed to be before you came into the earth plane. Connect with the moon and open yourselves to a different kind of healing energy and light, which will accelerate all you have been doing. Open to the changes! Keep focused on the positive aspects of life. Call on me to help with your connection to the moon and the divine feminine within.

Your life is changing daily! Do not be afraid, for wonderful experiences await you.

I send you blessings, love, light and encouragement to make the powerful connection with the moon and your divine feminine. Have a glorious, light filled day.

Forty-Nine

Aeracura

I come to you today bearing gifts from the universe. I am here to support you in receiving your gifts. Call on me when you need an emergency infusion of money and I will come quickly to aid you. It is important that you be willing to receive or you will block the gift. Focus with intention, willingness and receptivity and the gifts will be yours.

It is important that you learn to receive, for it is in receiving that you may help others to give and receive. Most of you on the earth plane who are reading this are people who are excellent givers and you give and give, with no thought of any reciprocation for the things you do and the things you give.

I am here today to tell you to learn to receive and accept the gifts with no thought, except to say thank you! Keep in mind that when you receive, you allow others the opportunity to feel as good as you do when you give. This applies to receiving everything, including compliments.

I see how many of you react when someone compliments you either on a job well done or something you said, or even how you look. Most of you have difficulty accepting the compliment and denigrate yourself even in a small way. Learn to say thank you, just thank you! Share with the person doing the giving the joy they have in giving to you.

Learn to receive from yourself! Set an intention daily to look in the mirror and offer love to your reflection. Accept the compliment from yourself about how important you are here and now. Accept the giving and the compliments. Allow others to share as you do. It is just as important for you to receive and now is the time to accept.

Move into a lightness of being that allows you to accept yourself and know that when you receive gifts of any kind, you deserve them. You deserve to receive all that Spirit and the universe have to offer. You deserve to give to yourself! The more comfortable you become in receiving, the more you can give to others freely. The more that you accept and invite the universe to share with you the more open you will be and the further you will move into your awakening.

Spirit wants nothing more for you than the best. We, as angels and deities, are awaiting your requests for assistance. Know that when you ask us for help we respond, because we are committed to serving! Do not ask and then doubt that you deserve a response. Stay focused on your desire and know that whichever one of us you called will respond. Be willing to listen and trust that your request is being answered. Know that you deserve to fulfill your desire and that you deserve our help. We will help you learn to receive.

Call on me and let's play together and share together. Allow me to give to you, so that I may share in your joy of receiving. It is time for you to awaken to the fact that many things await you when you are open to receiving, your heart expands, your connection deepens and you move from fear to trust.

We wish to share this with you, so open your heart, mind and accept all that you deserve! I send you love and gifts to encourage you to receive all that we wish to give. You are grand, glorious beings who deserve more than you have received thus far. Start today.

WE ARE HERE FOR YOU

Fifty

Archangel Raguel

⟨∾⟩

I come to you today to help you to see that you are not alone and your struggles on earth do not need to be. Most of you know we are here to support you, but for some reason you don't ask for assistance. We are here to serve you! It is our highest honor to serve you. You deserve our help.

Know that as we watch you struggle, we stand by and send light and love, but we cannot interfere or assist without your request, so all we can do is to just stand by, awaiting word from you. Our only role is to assist those who wish our help. You can take your information and call on us for all kinds of reasons.

Each of us can assist you in a variety of ways and if you are unsure which of us to call on, ask for the name of one you remember and then request assistance from that one, or ask that the one you called speak for you to the specialist. We work together to help you as you live your life. Remember to focus on that which is positive and when you face life's lessons and challenges, speak up and ask for help. You do not have to do everything alone!

Many of you see yourselves with responsibilities and it is

true you have them, but you have help if you will only realize that you deserve it. We can assist in all ways and help you to open to information that can ease your life's journey.

When you feel anxious, confused, disappointed or any other feelings, call on us, breathe deeply and accept that we are here for you. Whatever your dilemma, you can ask for help! We can support your strength, courage or faith. We can open doors to ease your way. Do not be afraid to ask for help. We always respond!

Our love for you is greater than you know. You are surrounded by love and we see your light sometimes dim from being overcome by fear, regret, anger and other lower energies. We can help you raise your vibration and look, with excitement and anticipation, to each moment of your life.

Know that beneath all that you pile on top of your shoulders, there is the light of Spirit. Do not carry what you see as your burden alone. You can change your life, you can be more than you envision.

Give yourself permission to be the great being that lies inside of you. We will help! We will gladly help you to move into the true you, which sometimes lies buried beneath a blanket of doubt, fear and helplessness.

Trust that you are meant to live your life freely and in joy. Trust that you are to bring your light to the earth plane, to assist others to live freely in light and joy. We will help! Whenever you need a boost, call on me I can and will joyfully assist you to relieve your burden and walk tall and free.

You are grand and glorious creatures and it is an honor to serve you! I, and others await your request. Please ask for help as you go through this time of transition. I await your call.

I send you blessings and love and offer to assist you in learning to accept the help that is waiting for you. Go with trust and joy into your day, knowing that we all support you in your growth and awakening.

Fifty-One

Athena

I come today to talk to you about standing in your power. What I mean by that is when you are in your power and you are secure in who you are, your attitude is open and compassionate.

You don't always have to be right! Allow others to be who they are and to have their own ideas and opinions! If you don't become invested in fixing everything, the need to control all is reduced.

When you stand in your power, you know what you know and you trust that what you know is right for you and your truth. This does not mean that you are not open to new ideas and opinions, but you are comfortable expressing your own ideas without fear. Your power comes from within and is intrinsic to your being. Know that you are powerful! Know that the power, of which I speak, is already within.

We see many of you giving your power away all the time. You give it to others, because you think they know more, or that they have the power to take away your income, or without them you are nothing. I say to you that you have all the power you will ever need, inside!

You give your power away when you allow others to dictate your behavior and beliefs. You give your power away when you let ridicule of your beliefs and opinions demean you. You give your power away when you stay in situations that are demeaning and abusive, out of fear that there isn't anything better for you. Now is the time to stop giving your power away!

Stand in your power! Stand in the knowledge that you are doing the best you can with the information you have. Know that you have the right to your opinions, beliefs, desires and mistakes. Once you accept these rights, you begin to accept the power. The power that you have has only been touched on the surface by most of you. Now is the time to move more fully into all that you are!

You are powerful in ways that you have only begun to awaken to. If you are unsure what I am talking about when I talk of power, think of a lion or a leopard; you can see and feel the power within these animals just by looking at them. They are comfortable in their power and it is evident in their walk and the way they carry themselves. Use this example and know that you are as powerful in your own right.

Release the fear and doubt that enfolds you and stand in your power and light! Know that you have the power to, at least, live your life according to your own terms, but know that your power is far greater than that. You are a creator! You are a healer! You are Spirit incarnate and as such, are capable of far greater things then you can currently imagine. Your power is far reaching when you allow yourself to be in it, comfortably!

I remind you of times when you are content within yourself and how people are drawn to you, when you are in that space of lightness and acceptance. When you are there, you are standing in your power; you have no doubts or fear! You are open to the world and look out with curiosity and enthusiasm, because you are not filled with anxiety and worry. You know that things will go as they are supposed to go.

Stand in your power now, today! You are powerful and by coming from your power, you give more to yourself, your family and friends and to the world. When you live in your power, you expand your world and invite new experiences and greater opportunities into your life. Live in your power and do what you came here to do!

We support you and offer our assistance in every facet of your life, from the small to the great. Call on us to help you live in your power so that all may benefit!

I thank you for reading this and with respect and honor, I offer my service to show you the way to your power. I send light, love and blessings to you all.

Fifty-Two

Brigit

I have come to you before and I come to you today to talk about supporting you and helping you with the courage to stand in your power. Yesterday, power was discussed and I am here to repeat "You are powerful!" I am here today to let you know that we support you, as you acknowledge the power that is within.

Call on me to protect you and to assist you with the courage to be the powerful being that you are. Know that your power is capable of great things and that most of you have only touched the surface.

I come to tell you that it is time for you to be powerful! I am here to tell you that any courage you need, to be who you are, will be supported by me and all others who wish to assist you to be all that you are. When you doubt that the choices you have made are correct, call on me to support you. When you disbelieve what you have created is really yours, call on me!

You are intuitive, clairvoyant, and capable of creating things with the power that lies within. Know that this power is available to you when you release the fear that your power will harm others. Know that this time you have come to use your power for love, not control. Know that the courage you need to be powerful is already inside you. I am here merely to support you. I am strong and fearless and will stand with you in whatever capacity needed, to help you be the powerful beings that you are. Be powerful now! Be courageous and take the steps necessary to open yourself to the power within. Let all that you are shine forth and accept that it is so!

Call on me and I will come and work with Archangel Michael to protect and assist with the courage that you feel you need. Do not fear, but accept and trust that this power is yours for the asking. Do it now!

I am honored to offer my service to you. With respect and love I send blessings and support.

Fifty-Three

Kuthumi

⌒⌒⌒

Today I speak of focus and determination. I offer you my support as it applies to every effort in your life. Call on me to support you when you wish to focus on your life purpose or enlightenment.

Many of you become distracted by worry and concern and instead of focusing on what you desire, you focus on everything that can go wrong. I exhort you to focus on positive outcomes. Remember, what you focus on is the energy that you send into the universe and it is what returns to you. If you focus on the fears and worry about the outcome, you will create obstacles in your path.

Call on me to help you focus. I will help you to release your fears and worries. I will help you focus your energies on the positive outcome you desire. Remember, everything is possible and it is not always necessary that you know how you will achieve what you desire. Just know that what you can dream, you can do and when you decide and affirm, it can happen.

I will help you to continue to affirm that which you wish to achieve and to release worries and concerns about how it will happen. It is not for you to know every nuance needed to achieve your goal. It is enough that you affirm and then follow your inner guidance toward that goal.

Do follow the guidance you receive in the form of intuition, dreams and ideas, which seem to come from nowhere! These are all ways that you are being guided in the direction to reach your goal.

Do not let others impede your progress; do not let others instill doubt and fear! Trust that you are on the right path and like a missile, you can make corrections, which could be considered mistakes; but as you make the corrections, you will continue on toward your goal.

You have the ability to create and do great things. Let your imagination flow with positive energy and release the outcome to the universe, knowing that when you release it and stop worrying, you will be ready to receive all you have requested.

With great respect and honor I offer you my assistance in creating positive outcomes in your life.

Fifty-Four

Mother Mary

I open my arms to enfold you and protect you. I wipe your tears and ease your fears. Feel my love for you, as I send it to sooth your soul. I send my love to totally enfold you and to fill you with warmth. I cheer for your successes and share your sorrows. I am here for you always! I expect nothing, except that you open your hearts to the greatness that is within you. You are lovable and worthy of your heart's desire.

You are all my children and I will help you always. I will not do your work for you, but I will intercede when you ask for my help. I am always available to you, just call my name and you will feel me with you to give you comfort and support. You can lean on me when you feel weary; and come to me to celebrate as I encourage your growth and awakening.

I see all that you are and all that you do. I see your weaknesses and strengths and I love all of you. Do not be afraid, for it is out of fear that you strike out against others and also against yourself. You are perfect just as you are!

Do not struggle so! Give your struggles to the angels and Spirit. Be willing to accept help with your burdens and they will be lifted. You deserve help! You are worthy of happiness and success. You are loved! Now is the time to love yourself!

I am here for you in all ways. I can help you to open your hearts, with joy and laughter, as you go through each day. I smile at some of your antics and wish to indulge you in little ways. I do wish the best for you, but as every mother, I encourage you to be responsible.

It is time for you to come forth and use your gifts. Accept that these gifts are yours, to be used in your unique way. I see that when you accept all that you are, you can do great things. Do not let fear block you or undermine your work. Love yourself as I love you! Know that my love will always be here, regardless of any mistakes you make.

I open my arms and my heart and send you love which, if you accept it, will fill you and surround you. Let me share your life, let me share my love; let me support you as I can. Just for today, relax and release your fears.

Just for today, play, smile, sing and feel the enchantment and exuberance which lies within! Celebrate your life and I will celebrate with you.

With great respect and love, I send blessings, encouragement and caring, as you move through your day.

Fifty-Five

Guinevere

Today I come to talk about romance and romantic love. I am here to assist you in your search for romantic love, both for those inside a current relationship and for those who have none and wish one.

I see that many of you are unsure of where to go and whom to trust. I will assist you with this. It is important that when you seek romance, you know who you are and accept that whoever is attracted to you, wishes you to be who you are and not give yourself over to them. I stress that you are unique; and it is that uniqueness that attracts someone originally.

Many of you become involved in romantic relationships and then try to please your partner by trying to become who you think they want you to be. I am here to tell you to remain in your truth. Romance can be part of your life when you are precisely who you are! Do not give away parts of yourself to please another, for then the relationship is based on a false premise. Be true to yourself and at the same time, be open and willing to accept another for exactly who they are.

You are all divine and part of the attraction between two people comes from that part of you. Romance is wonderful when two people find each other and revel in the similarities and differences each brings to the relationship. Open your hearts and share who you are!

Be true to yourself and to your love! Know that in many instances each of you has fears and doubts. Call on me and I will assist you to be open and sharing in the relationship. Know that the more complete you feel within, the more open you can be in the relationship, without any expectations that the other will fill in your empty spaces.

Approach romance with a light heart and an open mind! Allow it to unfold at its own pace and be at peace. Romance is wonderful; it brings a glow to your life, because it is an outward manifestation that you feel loved. Call on me to help you in this area.

Know that you can experience romance at whatever age. Be open and optimistic that if this is what you desire, I can help you find it. Be willing to receive as well as give, for romance is a two way interaction.

I send my love and blessings. Let love flower in your life and when you feel stuck, call on me! May your life be filled with love, light and romance. Have a romance with life today.

Fifty-Six

St John of God

❦

With great respect and honor, I come before you today to offer my services in relieving depression and dark feelings. Call on me and I will assist you in removing the illusions that keep you in despair.

Your minds are amazing things and when you involve the ego with the mind, the stories you can create are sometimes out of this world. You can take a small incident, interpret it in a negative way and then watch; as you focus on it, it grows all out of proportion in the negative. I suggest that the next time you worry about something that will happen in the future, you check within to find out how much your ego has created a major concern, with no basis in fact.

I love you and wish to share with you the joy that I see around you. Look around you with gratitude and appreciation for all that you have and all that you are!

Stop when you start to worry about something and think about what you are doing and how you can change the way you are looking at the situation. The sooner you can change your thinking about something, the sooner what you are thinking about will change. Realize that every time you begin to go into a negative thought pattern or depression, this is your ego talking. When you look at yourself and your life with gratitude and joy, you are coming from your higher self. You have the ability to change your feelings, by changing your focus!

Your life is a series of minutes, hours, days and even weeks when you choose to focus on certain things in a negative or positive way. I remind you that how you focus your energy creates what you have in your life. I know that this has been repeated and that there are times when it takes everything in your power to focus, even for an instant, on something positive. I tell you to take that instant to change your focus, even if it is for a short time!

See if you can smile inside, even for an instant. The more often you can change your focus, the more it will break the pattern of negativity and depression in which you find yourself.

Call on me and I will help! I am at your service. When I was on the earth plane, I derived much pleasure from serving others. This is another way that you can change your focus, by serving others. It is not everyone's way, but it will change your focus. I wish to offer my service to share my joy and delight in you.

I know that many of you think that you have no control over your depression and when you are depressed, I know it is difficult. Call my name and I will come to help you, even for a minute. You will feel my energy and my love and joy for you.

I am one of many who wish to offer service to uplift you and celebrate you. Ask and you will receive all the help you need. Trust that we are all here to help you move into your perfection. Open your hearts, open your eyes and trust that every time you ask for assistance you will receive it, regardless of the situation or your view of it.

Know that you can also help yourself by changing your focus and not allowing fear to create a major situation out of something minor.

I thank you for reading and hope that you go joyfully into your day. I offer my services and speak for others when I say, "Ask and you shall receive!" Trust that it is so.

Fifty-Seven

Horus

I bring you love from all of us today. I come to tell you that I can help you see with clarity into any situation you face and also into the future.

There are times when you doubt your own feelings about the truth of a situation or a person. I can help you to see the truth with a loving perspective.

I will also assist you with the courage to face the truth in your life and the courage to make changes, if necessary, for the highest good of all. I will come when you call me to assist with courage, truth and seeing the truth from love, rather than judgment. You are all courageous and truthful, but there are times when doubt and fear enter, and then things are not always clear.

Know that you have the truth already within and you only need to be willing to access it with a clear and loving eye. I realize that this can be difficult for some of you, because you have been raised in situations, which belie the truth as you know it.

Many of you sit in denial of the truth, which is in your heart about a specific situation. Some of you go through life in denial. Know that when you are willing to see the truth in any situation, you can bring it forth. If there is fear of facing the truth, call on me and I will assist!

Truth is an important part of releasing the veil that surrounds your life. Truth is an important place to come from when you deal with all aspects of your life. See yourself with truth and clarity! Do not negate the gifts you possess. When I speak of truth, I speak of the loving perspective in all. Grant yourself the truth about your goodness and your worthiness to receive all.

Some of you fear the truth about yourself, because you have painted a picture in your mind of imperfection, which you see as unlovable. Know that the truth about you is far more beautiful than you would expect. You are love, light and beauty; know that this is true! Call on me to help you see that aspect of you, as well as the less desirable aspects.

I see most of you focusing on the less desirable aspects, judging yourself as unworthy. Now is the time to see the truth of you and the love, light and beauty that you are! Change your focus just for today and celebrate you! They say "the truth will set you free" allow all truth to be present in you now.

I send blessings and let you know that I see the loving truth within you. Go in Grace.

Fifty-Eight

Saint Germain

I come today to talk to you about your gifts and abilities. You have all incarnated with gifts, which you committed to use during this lifetime to assist the earth plane during its vibrational shift. You are all capable of manifesting miracles and bringing healing and awakening to others. Know that within each of you is a unique gift, which is needed at this time. Go within and listen to what you can do now. I will assist in providing the courage you need to awaken, more completely, to who you are. You are all needed now!

Now is the time to take your courage in your hand, stand tall and commit to what you agreed to do. Say out loud that you commit to your divine purpose and state, with intention, that you are going to do what you agreed to before you came into this life! Your grace and wisdom are needed now!

Do not doubt that you have the gifts within you, to create whatever is needed now, both for yourself and the earth. Do not fear the turmoil that you see, for some chaos comes when new energy and light begins to unfold. The more that can be brought into the light, the more things can change for the better!

There is resistance to the changes and the old order is digging in its heels to retain that which it had. Now is the time to stay focused in what you desire to happen. Do not give into the fear, for giving attention to the fear and terror will only increase that which you do not want.

I realize many of you say, "It is difficult to avoid the fear and terror" and I say, "Call on me or any of the angels and ascended masters, to assist you in maintaining your focus on the light." It is especially important that you focus on love and light, for your world needs all of that it can get right now. Do not give in to terror! Stay focused and know that your focus will assist in more ways than you can understand.

I send you my support and love. Many of you are aware when I'm around. Be open and stay focused.

Fifty-Nine

Aiene

I come before you today with honor and respect for all that you are and all that you have done. I offer you my support in your efforts to connect with the all, especially the oceans, waterways, earth and trees. It is important for you to make that connection, as the healthier the earth is, the healthier the air you breathe and the water you drink.

Give of yourself toward protecting the environment and the animals that live in the wild. Give of yourself to honor what the earth provides. Do not be wasteful and be grateful that the trees and the plants help to provide the oxygen you breathe. You are blessed by all for the care you take of the earth.

The more you respond to the needs around you, the more you will receive in the way of health and beauty from the very environment in which you live. I applaud your efforts and wish to encourage you in this.

I also am here to assure you that what you do to protect your environment is appreciated by all who share it with you. When you speak to others about your concerns, do so with a light touch, so that others will be open to your ideas and not be defensive. You must all work together for the greater good.

Share your gifts with nature! Take time out of your busy schedules to spend some time in nature, connecting. Nature is bounteous and beautiful and the more that you honor her, the more you will be honored.

Connecting with nature on a deeper level can open you to a deeper connection with Spirit. Take time to look at and feel, the energy in nature. Open your ears and hear the music of the wind, trees and birds, as they share themselves with each other and you.

If you listen with an open heart, you can hear nature's orchestra performing some of the most joyous music. Take the time to appreciate all that nature has to offer. Connect with nature and feel the peace that emanates from each tree, animal, bird, waterway and blade of grass doing what they committed to do. Nature speaks to you and will share her secrets with you if you open your heart and your ears. Do this today!

I send you blessings and music from the earth. Go through your day with a song in your heart and appreciation for the air that keeps you alive.

Sixty

Babaji

I come before you today to encourage your direct communication with God. You are divine and need no assistance to communicate directly with God. You will always receive a response; you just need to sit still and listen. Realize that the response you receive may not always be in the form you expect, but you will always receive a response! Call on me if you are unsure.

Know that all you have to do to get my attention and assistance is to speak my name. I am pleased to see the growth in each of you. I am please to let you know that you have progressed beyond what you perceive. You all grow daily in your awakening. Many of you follow disciplines that lead you toward greater connection with the all. Continue to follow those practices. Know, however, that you can progress by staying open and focusing your intent on connecting with the all.

Open your eyes and look for the signs which are before you daily. Spirit acknowledges your intent to connect in various ways, not always in large panoramic scenes with color and fireworks. Some signs are very subtle and you need to stay alert for the response! Just know that there is a response!

You are all connected, as you have been told before. Now is the time to awaken to the connection. All of us in the other realms, support what you are about. We encourage every step you take and want you to know that we are ready to assist, whenever you request our help.

Listen to your heart and know that when you lead with your heart, you are increasing the connection.

Stay focused on your healthy desires and stay intent, knowing that you are already manifesting everything you need.

I send you blessings and support. You are connected, even though you may not be aware. May light, love and joy be with you through each of your days.

Sixty-One

Merlin

Today is a day for divine magic. I come to assist you in creating divine magic. I will teach you ways to create and use divine magic for yourself and others.

Know that I will only teach those who choose to use it for good. I realize that you are all saying, "That is the only thing I am interested in using it for", however, when you get totally wrapped up in the reality that you have created, you may occasionally wish to use it against someone or some situation. Do not allow the temptation to come to fruition!

Divine magic is very powerful and is one of the powers that lie within you. Know that all you need to do to learn about divine magic is to go within and be open when you ask for information about divine magic. If you doubt that this is the only thing you need do, call on me and I will assist you!

Know that when you call on me, I expect that you are ready to learn and I will insist that you open your third eye to begin to work with the information I send. I expect that you are ready and willing to do the work. Do not look at it as work. Look at it as furthering your enlightenment and growing in your knowledge of your connection with the all.

I will work with you to open your mind to the gifts, which you already possess. I will assist you in deciphering information that will appear as thoughts or ideas out of nowhere.

I am sure that each of you is capable of using divine magic in very powerful ways. I am pleased to offer my assistance and teachings. Know that you each deserve to awaken to this information. Know that I already say that you are ready to receive it. Trust that the information is within you, waiting to be discovered.

You are all powerful light-workers and powerful leaders. Open yourselves to the opportunity to learn about a powerful tool in your makeup. I am here, awaiting your call!

Let me lead you to a wonderful experience and a gift which can be used to clear away many illusions that keep you tied to situations that are unpleasant, depressing and painful.

I send you love, light and the wondrous information that you are all connected. Live in the joy that is your birthright.

Sixty-Two

Ashtar

I come to you to offer my assistance in reaching your full potential. I also am working to prevent your earth plane from nuclear war. I, along with others from the other dimensions, am working to come to a permanent solution for this issue in your three dimensional world.

My main concern today is to let you know that I am here to assist in removing the veil, which keeps you separate from your true reality. The more that you can be open to removing the veil, the more you can reach your full potential.

Do not fear that once you have removed the veil, you will not be able to relate to those who still exist in a three dimensional world. That is not the case. You will be able to relate, but it will be from a far different perspective, as you will see people with new eyes. You will be able to see beyond the petty differences, into the full connection that exists for all. You will see the uniqueness of each, but also the connection and the divine within.

Call on me to assist you as you grow toward who you were meant to be. Know that everything is inside of you already.

All the knowledge and gifts are already part of your DNA.

It is time for you to stop procrastinating and open to your potential, by acknowledging the gifts that you have! I realize that there is fear about this. I also realize that since the veil exists, you are not sure what your steps should be. Trust that you will be guided to what you are to do. Trust that we are all here to support and protect you as you grow into the best that you are.

Open to all that is being offered! Open to everything that lies within you and know that this is yours to claim, now! Do not be afraid; and if you are afraid, call on us to support you and assist you to release your fears.

You are all wondrous beings and those of us from other dimensions see your struggles and wish to assist you in smoothing your way on your earth plane. You are greater than you know; and now is the time to lift the veil and see the wonder that lies within you as you. Take off your blinders and celebrate each other's differences and similarities!

Call on us to assist you in this endeavor. You are loved by all. Start now to move into your full power!

I send you love and wish to convey that many of us are working beyond the earth plane to prevent nuclear war and to raise the vibration in your world. Know that as you grow into your full potential, you are also assisting in this endeavor. We celebrate your progress.

Sixty-Three

Mother Mary

I bring you love and compassion today. Know that you are surrounded by love and compassion. I see many of you chastising yourselves for not being perfect and failing to reach your own expectations, or what you think others expect of you. Know that you are perfect as you are!

It is time to show yourself the compassion you give to others. It is time to allow yourself to relax and enjoy the moment! It is time to know that you are exactly who you are supposed to be in this moment. I surround you with love and offer you my heart, to show you how to be compassionate with yourself. You need not meet anyone's expectations, not even your own, to be loved by me and Spirit. All you need do is just be. Allow yourself to feel what this is like, no judgments or criticism.

I see each of you as your own worst critic. Stop now! Learn that if you make mistakes, they are the ways that you learn. Often, what you consider a mistake is just a short detour along the path or a bump in the road. You are all too hard on yourselves.

Know that you already have the gifts within that you are trying to work toward. Know that you do not need to follow anyone's teachings or disciplines, other than what you know to be true within you, for you.

I see many of you following the prescription that others offer and when you don't do everything exactly as you have been taught, you chastise yourself and sometimes go so far as to call yourself a failure. It is time to stop this! It is time to take the information you receive in study and filter it through your own heart and do what works for you!

Do not stress about following someone else's rules and regulations. Accept the fact that what works for some, will not always work for others. Trust that you have the ability, within, to take information you receive and if it resonates with you, you will be able to use it with ease. If it doesn't resonate, take what you need from the information and let the rest go. Do not struggle so, to be like someone else! Be yourself! Know that you came into this life with a unique purpose and it is unlike anyone else's purpose.

Yes, you are all connected, but you are all unique as well; and it is time that you accept your unique qualities. Celebrate yourself and your gifts! Relax and enjoy exactly who you are today. Know that you may be in a different space tomorrow and that is all right.

Just for today, show yourself compassion and accept all that you are with grace and joy!

I wish to fill your heart with joy and love. If you could but see the glory that you are in this very instant, perhaps you would then cease to be so critical of yourself. Today, now, give yourself love and acceptance.

Call on me and I will assist you! I offer my support and love. Let me love you as you deserve to be loved. Feel my presence and receive my love; let it fill you, surround you and help you feel safe. Let your heart be filled with joy and send this love and joy out from your body, forming a cover around you. Know that as you do this, you share it with the world.

I send you my love and delight in the glorious being that you are. Receive my love with an open heart and feel it fill you with peace today. My children, you deserve all the universe has to offer. Open your hearts and receive.

Sixty-Four

Dana

~~~

Today's message is about worthiness, and deserving what you have, and what you wish to develop and have. You are all divine and you are all royalty. Now is the time to allow yourself to acknowledge this. When you know that you are divine, you can move forward with your divine purpose.

Now is the time to know that all of us in the other realms honor and respect you for the path you have chosen. To walk on the earth plane at this time is to be in the thick of things, as they say.

You are needed now on the earth plane, as the vibration transitions into another level. Honor yourself, your gifts and your talents! Now is the time to know that when you fully stand in your power, when you acknowledge that you are capable, you can affect those around you in a positive way and assist them to believe in their own gifts.

You deserve all that you desire! The abundant universe awaits your call. You are all capable of creating more than you will ever need in regard to money and possessions. Open your minds to the fact that you deserve to feel safe and you deserve to be comfortable with where you are now.

Now is the time to say to Spirit that you are ready to receive all that the universe has to offer. Commit to this belief! Do not go into your usual mode of fear and doubt about your worthiness. You are worthy just by being who you are.

Open your hearts and minds to the great ability you have to manifest anything and everything. Call on me and I will help to ease your fears about being worthy. I say onto you, "You can have what you desire without any qualifications!"

You are capable of manifesting great things which, in turn, will enable others to step into who they are. The more that you accept your gifts, the more open you are to receiving all that is offered and the more you will be able to help others. Now is the time to change your belief about who you are and what you deserve. Now is the time to receive, with grace, everything you deserve. Do not hold back from fear or doubt. Know that you are worthy, that you are divine and that you do not need to struggle so.

Know that we are all here to support you as you walk your path on the earth plane. See yourselves as royal and worthy. Step out of your fear and allow yourselves to be the royal beings you are!

Honor yourself today with something special. Do something for yourself that is unique and gracious; you deserve it! Today, celebrate you with a special treat, without doubt about whether you deserve it.

Release the guilt and fear! Give those feelings to the universe and have them transmuted into love and light. Today, ask for the help you need and know that you will receive it.

You are grand, glorious and divine beings and we celebrate you, always! Today is the time for you to celebrate!

I send you love, honor and blessings beyond your wildest dreams. Please open your hearts and receive all that Spirit has to offer - no limits, no fear, and no doubts. Every time you ask for help, it is there. Open to asking and receiving, without reservations.

Sixty-Five

Lakshmi

I offer my assistance in creating abundance in your life. I will help you find careers that will be fulfilling and lucrative. Wealth is something that many of you desire, but what you don't think about is that gaining wealth without doing something that you love, leaves you feeling empty. Wealth, in and of itself, is not fulfilling. However, wealth is not a problem; for most of you it is the opposite.

Most of you have some strange ideas about wealth, especially if you are involved in work that is either spiritually based or in a helping profession. I am here to tell you that, "This is a conflict that needs to be resolved within you!" Your belief that "you cannot make money when you are helping others" is a mistaken belief. We, in the other realms, want you to know that when you charge for your services, you move toward a position where you can do the work you love and help others on a full time basis.

Most of you keep yourselves in jobs or situations for security reasons and yet, fail to request even a living wage for the services you provide to others. I am here to support you in your desire to be paid what you are worth and to let you know that To request an even exchange for your services is what it is all about! Money has energy of its own, so when you accept money for your services it is an energy exchange between you and the person for whom you provided service.

It is time for all of you to realize that you are worthy of wealth and abundance in all ways. Call on me and I will help you find a career which will support your beliefs, is fulfilling and will create wealth beyond your wildest imagination; all of this, while living in a state of peace and joy. No more stressing about how you are going to pay your bills or if you will be able to finally quit the job you dislike.

I will help you serve others, if that is your wish, and to be comfortable financially. Do not rely solely on your mind. I do not want you to dismiss your mind totally, but I do want you to go within and know that Everything you desire is already within you, waiting to manifest into your physical reality!

Many of you are saying, "Yes, but I do 'affirmations' and I do 'visualize' and I do everything that I can think of to create wealth and a fulfilling life, but it doesn't work!" I hear you say, "I've heard all this before and I'm still stuck and I'm still worried and I still don't know if I'm doing the right thing!"

I say to you, "Look at these thoughts and what do you see?" Your beliefs that everything must be a struggle, money doesn't grow on trees, you have to work hard for your money and tension and stress are part of what it takes to earn a good living, are all things that affect your ability to manifest that which you desire. These beliefs are self limiting. These beliefs are what hold you back from having the life you desire!

Call on me and I will help you release these limiting beliefs, so that you can open your heart and trust that you are meant to share in the abundance of the universe. Trust that you are meant to live your life to the fullest in every way, because the more you live your life to the fullest, the more you can help others to find their way. Can you give up the worry, the despair and the fear?

I will assist you in releasing these feelings. Open your hearts and your minds to the all that you deserve, and be receptive! Trust that you already have, within you, everything you desire to manifest and that you are capable of manifesting this into physical reality. You are God made manifest, therefore, you are capable of co-creating whatever you desire. Call on me and I will help you.

I send you blessings, love and abundance in every facet of your life. I offer my assistance in creating an abundant joyful life. Just ask and know that I will come, with joy in my heart, to be able to help. It is my honor to serve you in whatever way I can.

Sixty-Six

El Morya

I come before you today to offer my protection and help you move into faith. Call on me to release your fears and doubts about who you are and why you have chosen to live on the experiment of the earth plane at this time. Call on me to help you when you feel vulnerable and under attack, via depression or anxiety. I will come and install shields within your body, so that you won't have to erect your own barriers as protection.

What I see happening with you, when you feel that you must always protect yourself, is that your body tenses and you spend a great deal of your time with your body in that mode. The longer you hold tension in your body, the more likely that, over time, you will begin to feel aches and pains, as the body can only retain the tension for so long without protesting.

Call on me and I can help you overcome your inner obstacles. I will gladly place shields in two areas inside of you, so that you will be able to ease your need to defend yourself, as the shields will work as a defense mechanism. These shields can be easily removed by your intention. These shields will not interfere in your life or in your ability to connect with Spirit or other humans.

I offer you this help so that you may live from a more open position, without fear or doubt. Call on me and I will appear and wrap you in my arms, surrounding you with love and protection.

If, at this time, you would like me to install the shields, I will do so. Each of you will receive shields unique to you. In placing the shields, I will help to release some of your inner obstacles, which will allow you to awaken, more completely, to the divine within.

Once the shields are in place, you will be able to lower your own armor and will then see the world with different eyes.

When you are ready and I have come, ask me for the shields. I will place one in front of your heart and one at your back, particularly in the lower back. These will be placed in these positions, as these areas tend to be the most vulnerable for you. You may feel the shields go up, but know that they will be easily removed by your request. They will, however, stay in place until you ask for their removal. Again, I say to you, "These shields are only here to help you, not to hinder!"

You do not have to defend yourself once these shields are in place, as they will defend and protect you, while at the same time allowing you to relax and enjoy freedom. Once the shields are in place, things which would bother you in the past, will no longer affect you. You will be more grounded and less affected by the energies around you.

I send you love and protection. Remember to call on me to assist you and relieve you of your constant need to protect yourself.

Sixty-Seven

Kuthumi

I offer you my support in focusing on your life purpose and your goals. Call on me to help you prioritize things that you need to do. I will help you to keep your focus as you go through your day. I will help to remove obstacles to your life purpose.

When you are feeling overwhelmed by everything that is happening and everything you need to do, call on me and I will help to smooth your way.

Know that much of what you stress about can be worked out in a peaceful manner, if you change your focus to that which pleases you and do each thing as you get to it.

Know that the time restraints that you place on yourselves are only established in your three dimensional world. You do have the ability to expand or contract time. Notice how when you are fully involved in a project, time can expand or how, as you say, time can fly.

Know that you have enough time to accomplish all that is needed, without tightening your body into a knot.

If you find that things are becoming too much, call on me and I will help to ease the way for you. I will help you to focus and to move peacefully through each project.

It is important to know that you always have assistance. Call on each of us to help you! You are not alone and you do not have to rely solely on yourselves. When you ask for help, it is important to allow the help to arrive. When you ask for help, you need to accept the help when it comes. Do not be surprised if it comes in a form you least expect.

We are here for you to assist in any way you need. Trust that you deserve the help and trust that your requests are answered, whenever they are made. You may not always be aware of how you are being helped, but if you are open to receiving the help, you will be surprised at how much easier your life will be.

You have all committed to a life purpose. Now is the time to understand that we all are here to help you along the way. We all want you to succeed in your commitment. You are all on your way. Ask for help whenever you wish. Those of us in the other realms have committed to serve you and it is our honor and pleasure to be able to assist you in any way necessary.

Open your hearts, open your minds, open your eyes and your ears and Ask for help. We are here to make things easier for you, but you have to ask. We will not interfere with your life in any way, nor can we help without a request from you. It is time to bring peace and joy into your life, for the more that you reflect peace and joy, the more that the vibrations of the earth plane will change in the same manner.

I send you thanks for asking and I wish to honor and love you through every facet of your life.

Sixty-Eight

Archangel Zadkiel

I come to you today to let you know that you can call on me for help in a number of areas. I shall work closely with you when you have lost something. I will assist you when you need to study and/or your memory needs a kick-start. I wish to bring laughter into your life and help you with compassion for yourself and others. Along with the compassion, I wish to tell you, "It is time to lighten your load and brighten your outlook!"

You all seem to spend a great deal of time under stress. It is time to ask for help from those of us who are awaiting your requests. I have to tell you, "It can be boring at times, just waiting for requests and not getting any! All right, not really boring, but I am here to serve and I do wish to be serving."

I know you all feel like you are being lectured about asking and receiving, but I am going to continue. You deserve help! You deserve as much compassion as you show others! You are not meant to live your life as one long struggle. Know that you can grow and become enlightened by laughter as well as struggle.

I offer my services and the services of all the ascended masters, angels, archangels and everyone who has committed to serve. Call on us. Do not be afraid to ask! Do not fear that you are unworthy. You deserve the best. You deserve our help in every area of your life. Ask for help and guidance and know that you will receive it without conditions.

You do not have to bargain to receive help. All you have to do is ask and then listen for the answer. You have been surrounded by help your entire life, now is the time to awaken and use the help that is offered.

As you know, you can't receive help if you don't ask! I leave you with this thought: Ask for help or guidance whenever you wish. Trust that you are receiving an answer if it moves you more completely along your path. We await your requests.

If you hear constant criticism, this is not from us! We support you in loving, caring ways, not critical ways.

I send you love, joy, laughter and the courage to ask for help. Celebrate your life and treat yourself, by having someone help you carry your load.

Sixty-Nine

Artemus

My message to you today is to trust your intuition and your power. You acknowledge your power by knowing, in your heart, who you are and trusting that the information you receive from within, is true. When you come from your power, you stand in strength and truth. It is the time that you are who you are meant to be.

When I speak of standing in your power, I mean that you are secure in who you are and in your beliefs and knowledge; it is when you accept that others have their own opinions and their opinions don't have to be the same as yours; it is when you can be open to all kinds of ideas and discern that which rings true for you.

When you are in your power it is that time when you accept that we are all connected and yet, unique; it is when you feel like you are connected to everything and yet, comfortable in your own physical self; it is when you know, without knowing how you know, that you are in the right place in time; it is when you can enter a discussion about anything, without needing to persuade anyone; it is when you stand firm in your beliefs and yet, accept that others beliefs may be different than yours;

it is when you can offer to help someone, if asked, without needing to impose your ideas on them or fix them as you think they need to be.

It is time to be in your power! It is time to realize that power doesn't mean controlling anyone. It is time to know that the power that resides within all of you must be brought forth at this time, so that the children may claim their power. The more comfortable you are in your power, the more that the children and others around you will be comfortable in their own.

Your power is what moves you to accomplish things and to make a difference. Love yourselves and accept the power that is within. Use it with wisdom and help to move this earth plane to a different level, where all people live in harmony and peace, acknowledging that everyone is powerful and each is divine.

I send you blessings and celebrate you as the powerful beings you are.

Seventy

Archangel Ariel

I come to you to offer my assistance in any way that you can use help. My name means "Light of God" and I can assist in a variety of ways. As you go through your day, know that all you have to do is call my name and I will be there for you. I can help you clarify a situation and seek the truth.

As you all go through your day, I see that you are beginning to realize that help is there for the asking and I speak for all when I say, "We are happy to see this!"

You are glorious beings and it is time to again know that needing help does not take anything away from you and your abilities; asking for help, will only extend your time to grow into the knowledge of your abilities.

Your light shines daily, although some of you have light that is clouded by fear and doubt. Know that you need not go anywhere or do anything to receive the light. The light is within you! It is time to awaken to this!

By asking for help, even in this area, you do not diminish what or who you are. You will receive help and then you can open yourself more completely, without being weighed down by problems you perceive in your life.

I come to tell you that when you are ready to loosen your need to control everything in your life, you will awaken to the glorious world around you. You will begin to accept our help as an extension of you and your gifts, rather than weakness.

Now is the time to remove the dark glasses that you wear and see the glory that is you. Now is the time to ask for all the help that is awaiting you, for in the asking, you will receive and you will change your view of the world around you and of yourself.

We see each and every one of you as filled with strength and light. Know that you may live more fully in this strength and light, by asking us to assist you in relieving your fears, doubts and anything else that prevents you from fully experiencing your true self.

We are here for you! We will help you in every way, to awaken to knowledge that lies within; to awaken to the glory that is you; to awaken to the great influence you have on those whose lives you touch; to awaken to joy, love and the compassion toward yourself and others, which lies within you. Ask us and be open to receive, so that your changing vibration will assist the earth plane and yourself to be everything you are meant to be.

I leave you with love and my sincere offer of assistance in every facet of your lives. Live each day with joy and laughter and call on us to help you maintain this way of life.

Seventy-One

Athena

I come to you today to talk about your ability to command the energies of the universe to work for you. You have the power and the right to command, rather than just ask that all of the energies around you work for you. Command that the wind or the stars or the clouds work with you to do what you wish!

Do not fear the word command. It is a form of prayer, however, in the command form you come from the position of power, rather than seeking. You have the power to command! Use this wisely and with compassion. If you are unsure of how to use this ability, call on me and I will be pleased to assist you. I can show you how to command! I command the energies of the universe regularly to work with me.

As you know, everything is energy and, as such, many things can happen with a small movement of the energetic force. Use your power to move the energetic forces, by commanding of them what you wish! Know that you have the power and by using this power with grace, poise and wisdom, you can move mountains.

Do not fear the power that lies within. Do not fear that you have no control over this. You have the power. You have the ability to stand in your strength and create reality as you wish. Do not fear that you will use this power against others. When you are cognizant of your power and the great ability that you possess, you can use it to create a better reality for yourself. Use your abilities!

Awaken to that which lies within and accept the responsibility that is part and parcel of your power. Now is the time to awaken! I will guide you, if you ask. You are supported by all in your awakening, as your responsible power is needed now! Do not fear you will be fully and completely supported in your efforts.

Be who you are, now! This is not something you have to study. It is not something outside of yourself. You already have all that you need, within! Awaken now and allow this strength and power to support you in your life purpose, without doubt or fear. Do it now.

I send you my support and love. I offer you my guidance, as you transition into your awakened self.

Seventy-Two

Ishtar

Today I offer to send you light, which will surround you and deflect the lower energies of fear and doubt. You can call on me at any time to shine the light of love and healing upon you, so that you can release all the fears and doubts in your life. I will assist you in this process, so that you may be in the light of love and fearlessness.

You are loved and you need not live in fear and doubt! Take my hand and know that I stand with you to support you in all your endeavors. I support you as you develop and work with the gifts and talents within. I will shine the light down on you and surround you, so that you will be free to pursue your divine purpose.

See the light and know that you are safe. Feel the light and know that you are protected and that the fear, with which you have been engulfed, is disappearing. As you stand within the light, you will be able to allow your own light to shine forth, breaking the darkness and spreading the light into the world around you.

Use the light that I send and send your own light out to reach into the corners, where darkness runs to hide. Like a candle in a darkened room, your light will fill the area and reduce the fear, doubt and anger in any situation. I will assist you in this effort!

Know that the light I shine, dear ones, is open to receiving love and that it only deflects that which is of a lower vibration. Stand in this light and lift your vibration, opening to the love that surrounds you within and without. You are loved! You are worthy of love! You deserve to live fearlessly and free.

Be free, be strong and stand tall in your glory! Stand in the light I send and know that you are already perfect as you. You are loved and supported. Fear not, for even if you make a mistake, this will not remove the love. Be prepared to receive love, as it will empower you and provide you with the wisdom to move through life with compassion and grace.

I send you the light today, when you ask. I await your request. Go through your day with strength, wisdom and love in your heart and soul. Be free.

Seventy-Three

Maitreya

I am often called the "Laughing Buddha." I am always depicted as the "Laughing Buddha." I share my laughter with the world. Picture me and rub my belly for luck and laughter! I speak today to tell you it is time to spend the day in joy and laughter. Lay aside your worries and cares for today and spend time laughing and enjoying yourselves.

As you know, laughter brings you closer to Spirit. It increases your vibration and when you laugh you breathe in the all. Share your laughter, share your smiles and share your love of life today with everyone! Look around you at the glory that is there! Spend time around little children and listen to them laugh, from the depths of their souls. They do this, because they operate in the now.

When you laugh, you are truly present in the moment. When you laugh, you share with others a lightness that expands to fill the room. Laughter can bring release from worries and stress; it helps your heart and your mind; it truly can heal you. Laughter is a joyous sound and is contagious. Take today and share your laughter and your light! Take the time to share a joke or a smile and brighten, even for a minute, your day and the day of someone else. Laugh, sing, hum or just smile and lighten your day! I send you laughter and joy. Picture me and my round belly, laughing! Rub my belly in your imagination and I will share my laughter with you. Enjoy the day!

Seventy-Four

Ganesch

I am here to help you remove obstacles in your path. I see many of you being held back by the problems in your life. What many of you know is that it is your mind that creates these obstacles! I know that this is often a hard concept to fully grasp, as most of you are unaware of the power that you have. Know that even the problems in your life are illusions, which can be removed.

All of the obstacles in your life can be removed by releasing the fear, which keeps you stuck. I can hear you now saying, "But, how can that be? I want to move more completely into my divine purpose, but there is this problem or that problem, none of which were created by me!" I say to you that you create your life, not necessarily on a conscious level, but you have the power.

Your beliefs hold many of you back from achieving and receiving all that you can. Do not doubt that your abilities are far greater than you know!

I will help remove the obstacles which prevent you from reaching your goals and desires. I will assist in puncturing the "balloon of illusion", which keeps you in your current position. I will help you change your beliefs and become motivated and active in participating in your life, as opposed to sitting on the sidelines.

You have the power and the strength to change your beliefs and to bring into your life all that you desire. Drop the illusion that you are not worth it and the thinking which states that you are under a dark cloud.

Change your affirmations from being merely statements, to full feeling, thinking statements, which are filled with the knowing that what you are affirming is already manifesting for you.

Call on me and I will assist you in these changes! When you affirm something, observe what happens in your mind and your insides. See how it feels and what your mind puts in as an attempt to doubt the ability to manifest the affirmation. You may be surprised! When the doubt occurs, look to the belief which generated it and once it has been brought to the surface, you will be able to release the limiting belief.

Today when you affirm, call on me to help you. I am at your service! I, cheerfully, remove obstacles, as it is my great pleasure to watch you achieve and bloom.

I bring you love, laughter and help in removing obstacles. Go forth today with a light heart, knowing that you will have all the help you need.

Seventy-Five

Archangel Chamuel

I come today to talk to you about grounding yourself in who you are. I see many of you wandering, hither and yon, not really sure who you are. Know that to discover who you are you must go within! I can assist you in this journey. I am one of the archangels who can help you find lost items, including the lost you. I can assist you in this process.

Some of you look outside of yourself for the answer about who you are; you can be assisted in uncovering your deep-self by this method because in conversation with another, ideas are exchanged and what is often hidden within is brought into the light to be acknowledged.   I do caution you about some of these methods, as I see you begin to focus your energy on what has been discovered, instead of looking at what has been revealed and then releasing it. I say this to remind you that what you focus your energy on is what you bring into your life. I understand that this can be a difficult concept to work with, but understand that you are very powerful beings and to use a statement from your plane, "What you think is what you get!"

Another statement which is a good reminder is that "Energy

flows where attention goes!" so bring the hidden information into the light. Acknowledge it and then release it. Accept that it has affected you and change what has affected you into a belief which brings joy and affirmation into your life, instead of dwelling on that which created pain. Let it go and if need be, move through the pain created by the information and then release it! Do not expend a great deal of time with it. Take the time you need, but call on me to help you recover the joy that was you prior to the creation of the pain. Focus on bringing that feeling back into your life! I will help you. I will help you stand in your truth and know who you are, in comfort and love. Call on me and I will assist you in finding yourself.

Once you are on your way, you will then stand on a stable platform from which to move yourself in many directions. Go within as well as without, to discover the glory that is you. Seek beyond your tendency to criticize yourself. Seek into the depth of your soul and look with wonder on the being that you are, unique and yet similar to everyone.

Celebrate that which you present to the world as you and celebrate that which you protect as you. Celebrate you! You are glorious and I wish to offer my services to assist you in discovering this. Be open and accepting! Do not fear what you have yet to discover about yourself, for I say to you, "It is far greater in glory than you can imagine and far less filled with darkness than you believe!"

I leave you with the request, Call on me as you go through the discovery process and I will assist you. It is a wonderful journey and I would be honored to help you along the way.

Seventy-Six

Apollo

I come before you today to bring you light. I offer my assistance in healing for any problem you have on any level. I am strongly connected with the sun and, therefore, bring this light with me, whenever I am present. When I am here you may feel the heat of the sun, even on the darkest days. Take the time to connect with the sun's energy and call forth the healing rays. I will work with you to release and cleanse all illness and disease that you are experiencing. Although I am connected with the sun, I offer you this:

You are also connected to the sun and, as such, can create with the sun, a healing energy which can be used to assist others when ill health or depression takes hold. I will assist you!

You have the power, within you, to heal yourself and others, by calling on the energy of the sun, the moon and Spirit. When you work with the energies, you do not deplete your own energy and at the same time, you send a variety of healing to whatever area is in need. Know that you can call on me! Know that I am available to lend you my powerful presence and energy, to work with you in the area of healing and light. I will bring light, whenever you need it! Do not fear that you will not see it or feel it, as this is very powerful and when you are open to receiving, it will come.

The sun can assist you in raising your vibration and increasing your comfort in healing. You will affect others with a positive energy, just by being in their presence. Connect with the sun! Feel the heat and the golden rays, filling your being with light and energy. Take them into yourself and sit in this energy, whenever you begin to question whether life is worth the effort. When you are in this energy, it will lift you up and help you open your eyes to a new day and a new way of thinking. Take the time today to connect with this powerful energy! Take it in and let it express through you, as you allow the moon and other energy to express through you. Everything is connected and by combining all the energies in certain situations, you create an unusual and powerful healing.

Not every situation calls for this type of energy. Trust that you will know when to use it, or if, in doubt, you can call on me and I will let you know.

I send you blessings and the rays of the sun to lighten your day and bring you new energy for whatever you need. Ask and I will come.

Seventy-Seven

Dana

I come before you today to speak of the joy of receiving. You are givers and caretakers, but now is the time to receive with joy and gratitude! You are all willing to go out of your way to assist others and this is good, but you need to receive as well.

You deserve all the help you need and all the abundance of the universe is at your feet, waiting to manifest when you accept that you are deserving. Receive with joy and a song in your heart!

Do not doubt that it is right for you to be on the receiving end of gifts and treasures. The universe is abundant and gifts await your request. Know that you are capable of creating everything you desire. I shall be your support!

As the energies of Spirit weave through and around you, know that I am here to help you accept that you are a deity in your own right. Sit with this thought! Feel how it is to be royal and powerful, even if it is only for a moment. The more you take the time to feel your own powerful, royal self, the more you will accept this in your mind.

I understand, for most of you this can be a difficult concept to accept, as you have been taught that you are less than. Your religious training teaches that you are born sinners and I say, "This is a belief that has created many of the problems you face in your life today!"

What has been written and taught to you does include information about your ability to produce miracles, but this information is not the focus of the teachings. The focus of what you have been taught is that you are sinners and unworthy!

Throughout the history of the earth plane, there have been many who wish to control others and some have chosen to do this through organizations that teach about Spirit. As we have observed in the other realms, what you learn and what seems to take hold from these teachings is that you are unworthy. Think about what this does for you. I say, "You are all miracles and you are all royalty!" Now is the time to allow this to penetrate your heart. Your soul knows this, but has been unable to overcome the years of teaching that have enveloped your being.

Now is the time to acknowledge the greatness within you. You are needed now, to lead by example! Call on me and I will help you focus, even for short periods, on the glorious Spirit within. I will help you receive, with joy and tranquility, all that you deserve. You can perform miracles now! Accept who you are in truth and happiness! Accept that you are more than worthy. You deserve everything the universe has to offer. Lift your hearts and minds and know that anything you can imagine, you can have, or be, or do, for you are greater than you know and certainly capable of what Jesus said, after performing a miracle: "You are all capable of doing this, or greater!" Now is the time to believe this! Now is the time to change your belief of unworthiness, to a belief that you deserve all! Fear not, that you will be selfish!

Know that when you open to this change in belief, you not only receive yourself, but you are willing to give more to others and they, in turn, will do the same, for the fear of lack will have disappeared.

Call on me and I will support and help you as you change your focus. You are royalty! Believe, feel and know that this is true!

I send you love, stars and royal garb, so that you may know, in your hearts, your greatness.

Seventy-Eight

Archangel Raziel

I am here today to offer you my help in discovering your gifts and talents. I will help you access esoteric information, which can only be obtained by going within. You are all gifted with psychic abilities and when you call on me, I will help you awaken, more completely, to these gifts.

I can provide information about ways in which to manifest. I am known as the archangel who knows the "secrets of God." I will teach you many things, if you wish to learn. I am here to tell you that now is the time for you to open to that which is within!

You are all gifted with many abilities in the areas of healing, clairvoyance and many of the other esoteric fields. Now is the time to open up to these abilities. You are needed now!

Now is the time to lead the way to a new way of communication. Your vibration is rising and you are connecting in new ways daily, both with one another and with the other realms. Call on me and I will guide you along this path.

Fear not, for you have chosen to be here on the earth plane at this time, to lead the way. You are all capable of this commitment you made, when you were on the other side.

Questioning why it is happening at this time of your life? Know that this is the time the earth plane is ready to receive the changes that are happening! You have chosen to contribute your light and your vibration to assisting in these changes. Call on me! I will help you to be comfortable in your role. Now is the time that the earth plane is going through changes. Now is the time that it is important to stay focused on love and compassion toward everyone and everything.

Do not get caught up in your illusions of fear and other lower energies. Stay focused on the higher energies, knowing that the more you focus on higher energies, the more you will provide the example for others to do the same. I say to each of you, "You are important in this changing time!" It is precisely what is happening at this time, which is the reason you are here, now! Know that you have the strength and the ability to use your gifts to lead those around you. Do not doubt that you are strong and powerful.

Open today to all that you have within! Release fear and doubt and step forward, so that others may awaken to their own light. Now is the time! Do not hesitate, because you feel you do not know enough, or you are not capable. You have everything you need within and much has been provided, through the teachings of others who have gone before.

I say to you, however, "Trust the information from within, which is filled with joyous light and love." If you hear echoes of fear and terror, know that this is not what is happening. The changes taking place are bringing your earth plane to healing and peace. Keep your focus there! Lead the way and increase the vibration around you!

You are grand, glorious beings whose light, energy and love

are needed now, as part of the greater plan.

I send you love and light, offering my services to assist you in your awakening to the powers within.

Seventy-Nine

Lakshmi

I come to you to offer my services with abundance and prosperity. Now is the time for you to know that it is all there for you! Know that you are worthy to receive and open your hearts to receive all the universe has to offer.

Do not doubt that you deserve to receive. Stop qualifying each request you make. It is time to receive for yourself, without concern for anyone else. You have all lived your lives with concern for others. Now is the time to be concerned with yourself and receive all the joy, laughter, peace and prosperity that the universe has to offer.

Do not be afraid about asking for something just for yourself. Do not feel that you are being selfish when making the request. Know that it is time to change your beliefs about prosperity and wealth.

We, in the other realms, see the struggles you go through and we wish to help you change your beliefs, so that things such as prosperity and opportunity will flow to you more easily. Call on us to assist you! Our help is always available, but you have to get out of our way after you have made the request. What I mean by this is: When you ask for help, release it into the hands of whomever you made the request. Do not worry about any aspect of the request. Make the request and then let it go! You will find that you will begin to experience ideas and guidance, which will help bring your request into fruition. Do not question your request, or whether you deserve to even make the request.

Know that you have the right to receive everything the universe has to offer. Now is the time! Release yourself from the shackles, which bind you and prevent you from receiving everything. Do not live by the rules which have been instilled by a society that is only comfortable with maintaining the status quo.

It is time to spread your wings and fly! It is time to allow yourself to know how much your efforts contribute to the overall growth of your earth plane. It is time to reward yourself for all you do. It is time to allow Spirit to give to you.

We all await your requests, with open hearts and joy, in helping you receive all that you deserve and more. Spirit is calling you to open and receive! Now is the time!

I send you blessings of love, joy and prosperity. Ask for our help and lighten your load, knowing that the prosperity you desire will ultimately help everyone.

Eighty

Archangel Raphael.

I am here for you any time you call. I am here to heal physical disease on every level. I heal more than the physical problems. I work in a holistic manner, so that we can get to the source of the problem. Know that all you have to do is call on me and I will come. Know, also, that I will not interfere in your life without your permission.

You can call on me and send me to be with others, but unless they give me permission to work with them I can only be with them and not take an active role in their healing. I say to you, "When you ask for my help, I will be there for you!" I say that when I am involved in healing of any kind, you may put away your doubt and trust that things will change, for the highest good!

I want you to know that when I work with you in your healing, you take an active role, but I add my help, which in many instances speeds the healing process. You have a major part to play in any healing that takes place. You are the catalyst and I am the energy that works in conjunction with you, to affect all aspects of your being. I work to heal, completely, all aspects that affect the disease you wish to cure.

Watch your thoughts in the process of the healing. Be aware of where you are placing your focus. Know that the more you can experience the changing patterns in every area of your being, the more involved you are in it. I tell you this not to push you to try, but to be aware of where you are focusing and how you are using your energy!

In the healing process it is vital that you take care of yourself in all ways! Many of you ask for healing and then continue to push yourselves to the limit of your endurance and beyond. An important part of the healing process is to honor yourself! Listen to what your body is telling you. Take the time to acknowledge that the pain you feel, or the spot you see are signs to let you know that it is time to care for you.

What do I mean when I say, "You play an important part in the healing?" I don't mean that you are to expend extra effort. I mean that you are to take the time to care for yourself, in all ways. You must allow yourself the time to heal. You must take the time to be. Treating yourself wisely and lovingly at all times will help to prevent serious illness.

Listen to your guides as they come to your aide. Trust your intuition as it guides you in the care of your physical, emotional and spiritual self. Be aware that it is important to always honor your being! It is always important to take care of yourself first, so that you will have the energy to care for others! If you do not care for yourself first, you will have nothing left to give to others. You are your first priority, which is as it should be.

Know that you are given grace to heal any problem or any disease, when you ask for it. Know that by taking care of yourself, you are not acting in a selfish manner, but doing what is for the highest good of all. When you are cared for and healthy, you can provide more for those around you and those who count on you. Again, I offer my help!

Know that it is my pleasure to assist you in all ways. Know that when you ask me to assist, I will be with you, throughout, and will happily and joyfully help you heal. Trust that you are worthy of my care and know that it is with great love, that I am here for you. Open your heart and mind, and allow me to do what I do best for you, as I do for others.

I am present for you, in all ways that may help you live your time on the earth plane in a healthy way. I am honored to serve. Call on me whenever you need me.

Eighty-One

Archangel Jeremiel

I come today to offer my services to help you see the future. I know that you have questions about your future and the future of the earth. I will assist you in looking into the future, basically, so that you will have an idea about what your next step is to be and to help you stop worrying about what is going to happen.

Know that you are all capable of envisioning the future. You all have the ability to see what needs to be done and to take it upon yourselves to do this. Know that what you see is always open to change and that you might see something that will give you an idea about what needs to be done to either change what is happening, or to expand it. Do not fear that a vision of the future is set in concrete! It is flexible and, as the wave in the ocean, can change with a change in vibration, either through a change in the vibratory rate of the humans, or the vibratory rate of the earth plane.

Have no fear about your future! It is open to your interpretation and you are in control of your life. You have the ability to change your life, today! You can see you future and know that this is not necessarily the future exactly as depicted. You are the creator of your life and you can change what you have ahead of you, by changing your actions and your beliefs.

When we work together to see into the future, it will provide you with an opportunity to make different choices from those you might have made, had you not seen the future. What happens is that you are following a certain path and you may continue on that path until something happens and you have the opportunity to, perhaps, see things in a different way, or to be in a different place. Fear not that you will hate what is in the future! You can change everything. When you take the opportunity to see, you can take the opportunity to change!

I will help you to open your eyes and to see what you can do as a next step along the way. Today is the time to step into the future and be who you really are. I give you my help and blessings in this grand adventure.

Eighty-Two

Dana

As we have discussed before, you are all royalty, but you live as though you do not deserve anything but trials and tribulations. You live with guilt, as you have been taught by the various systems in your earth plane.

Know that guilt is one of the lowest energies and if you focus on it, it will keep your vibration in a very dense place. Guilt is an interesting phenomenon, as most of you don't even know why you feel guilty; it just is something that infects your life from time to time. I say, "There is nothing to feel guilty about!"

I shall assist you in releasing the guilt in your life, so that you can raise your vibration and create abundance, joy and blessings in your life. Do not allow guilt to take hold of your mind and heart! You can release it, by changing your focus. When you analyze the cause, bring it into the light and then release it!

Do not spend your time and energy on guilt, as it will take hold and lead to depression and a sense of unworthiness. Guilt does not have to ride in your back pocket, or anywhere else in your life. Guilt has been used by those who wish to control you and I will say that it has been a very effective tool.

It is time to stop buying into the idea that you have anything to feel guilty about! You are in the human experience and mistakes have been made as you travel your path, but a mistake is nothing to feel guilty about. This feeling of guilt has been instilled, in most of you, at an early age in your earth plane existence and now is the time to eradicate it from your life!

Know that any decision you make is based on the information you have. Know that the choice is yours, to live in guilt and fear or to release even the word guilt from your life. Guilt serves no purpose, except to keep you in place; it denies who you are and prevents you from following your divine purpose. In some instances, it prevents you from even looking for your divine purpose, as you feel you don't deserve anything except sorrow and misery. Release these thoughts!

Call on me and I will help you change your focus so that you may see, if only for a moment, the royal beings you are and feel the joy and light which live in you. Step out into the light! Drop your cloak of guilt today, NOW, without fear of reprisal and experience the lightness and joy, which can be a permanent part of your life.

Do not fear that if you release the guilt, you will be punished. You have been punished by carrying this guilt far too long. It is time to cut the chains of control, which others have used to keep you in your place. Stand up and let your true being shine forth into the world, today! "Guilt, be gone!" is something we can say together. Give it to me and let yourself be free.

Know that freedom is your rightful place and it will open you up to accept all the universe and Spirit have to offer. Today is the day to let go of any thoughts of guilt.

Let your vibration expand and grow and when you feel yourself falling back into feeling guilty, change your focus with your mind and call on me to assist you in releasing the feeling of guilt. I will help you to look at any situation in a different way, so the old, lower energy of guilt will not rear its head. Accept this as your birthright! Be free of guilt and you will have a new experience, which will increase your desire to never feel guilty again.

Know that you are divine and as such, have no need for guilt in your life. Awaken and be free! I send you love and offer my help in releasing any guilt left in your life. You deserve the best and guilt is an old pattern, that doesn't suit you anymore.

Live your life in freedom, joy and laughter! We all support you in this.

Eighty-Three

Artemis

It is time to know your inner self. I offer my services to assist you in realizing your authentic, natural self. I will help you tune into your intuition and live your life from the power and wisdom, which lie within. Know that you are valuable and now is the time for you to live from that place of truth, without fear.

Men and women are each imbued with feminine power, it is the creative force. When you acknowledge that this is a truth within you, you can begin to access it and use it to your benefit and the benefit of all.

It is an important period in the evolution of your earth plane and the more humans who operate from their authentic self, the healthier it will be. Do not fear who you are! Know that you are needed now and trust your intuition to assist you in following your divine purpose. You have much strength and power. Now is the time for you to live from that position. Know that you are safe and protected as you blossom into your true nature. Call on me and I will assist you in this process.

The world awaits your true energy and your gifts. Listen to your heart and go within, to know the truth. Do not fear that you are unworthy! You have much to offer and now is the time to use your gifts and talents to the fullest. Know that you have much information to share and that information is needed now!

Do not fear the transition and changes, which are happening now. Much is being brought into the light, so that it may be made whole. The more that the lower energies are brought into the light, the less power they have.

Stand tall in who you are, as you are an integral part of bringing light to your earth plane. Live in your authentic self and allow your wisdom and intuition to guide. Share your knowledge and your light, without fear! The more authentic that you can be, the more that you will help at this time. Call on me and I will help you!

I send you love and blessings and I see you taking great strides to be strong in who you are. Keep up the motion and know your own powerful self.

Eighty-Four

Hathor

I can come to your aid in so many ways, that I am said to have "divided into seven goddesses" and therefore, am often referred to as "The Hathors." I offer my assistance in what ever area you need help. Today, I wish to speak of living your life as your heart desires. Many of you feel that you wish to live your life as your heart cries for, but you hesitate when it comes to making decisions that will lead you in that direction. I come to you today to offer my help in listening to your heart and mind about how you wish to live your life. It is time! You are ready to make your decisions after listening to the information, which comes to you from within.

I will assist you in tuning in, so that you may hear all that is there for you. It is time to live your life as you desire, without fear and trepidation that the world, as you know it, will fall apart. Know that what is in your heart, is there because it is a life that can be supported for the highest good of all. Know that by making decisions, which move you in the direction of your heart's desire, you empower yourself and others to become greater than they realize.

I can hear you saying that you are unsure what your true

heart's desire is or how you really wish to live your life. I say to you, "This is OK!" I offer my help, so that you may tune in and really listen to how you wish to live your life. You do not have to make any radical decisions and changes all at one time. You can do this in a gentle way. Just know that every decision you make affects how you live your life. It is time to live it with joy and peace!

The more you focus on your true feelings about your life, the more you will discover that the changes that take place bring you closer to a sense of joy. Know that you do have a grand design inside about how you wish to live.

The universe and Spirit support you in this desire. Start today to go within and ask yourself how you wish to live your life. This time, listen for the answer, for it may surprise you. This time, when you hear the desire, know that it is obtainable, as everything you can imagine, you are capable of manifesting. I can help you in your efforts! I do ask you to listen, but I also ask that you not try so hard.

When you make a decision do your work, then get out of the way so that Spirit and those of us in the other realms can do our work to bring about that which you desire.

Worry does not contribute to the outcome. In fact, it slows the process, so watch your focus! After you have made a choice and done your part, spend time relaxing and enjoying yourself; leave the rest of the work to us! You ask for the help and then try to do it all yourself. This is unnecessary! We do come to your aid, when you ask.

It is interesting to observe how you respond, when what you have asked for help with comes to fruition. You are often amazed and yet, the next time you ask for help, you doubt that it will come. I repeat, "Ask, do your part and then relax and we will do the rest!" A suggestion as a way to let us do our work would be to change your focus, rest, enjoy, laugh and let the outcome be as you have requested. Do not stop the flow by continuing to worry it to death!

I will help you change your focus. I will help bring more joy and laughter into your life, after you listen to your heart and mind with regard to decisions about your life.

Trust that when you make a decision that moves you closer to the way you really wish to live your life, you are supported on all levels. I will guide you in this search in a gentle and loving way. Now is the time to do the search, but to also sing, dance and enjoy the process, without worry about the outcome. I send you music, laughter and joy as you go through your day. Know that with each joyful expression and true laughter, you open more completely to the divine within.

Go forth today with joy in your heart, knowing that you are supported in every way.

Eighty-Five

Archangel Michael

I come today offering my love and protection. I offer my protection, because I see much fear among you. Do not let fear get a foothold in your life, as once you allow it to take hold, it becomes where you focus your energy and that only increases the fear! It is important to realize that the more you fear, the more that fear is projected into the world and the greater the number of people living in fear, the more this energy encompasses the world you live in.

I know that with all of the upheaval going on in your earth plane, many of you ask, "How is it possible to live without fear?" I say to you, "Call on me and any of the other angels and ascended masters you are comfortable with, and ask for their help. We are here for you!"

I will cut through your cords of fear and release you from the lower energy that engulfs you. Rise up and change your focus! You are needed now, to change the focus of your earth plane. I will protect you and support all that you do to encourage a positive shift in focus.

As has been discussed, much that is happening today is a part of bringing the lower energies to the light, so that they can be transmuted into love. Change your focus today! Open to the abundant universe and project that energy into the world, rather than the energy of fear. Realize that part of what is happening, is a result of the energy you are sending into the world, gathering together in a collective whole. If each of you changes your focus and lives from a joyful, loving energy, this is what will be projected and as such, will affect others, who in turn will affect others, and so on, and so it expands.

Today, live from love and celebration of all! Today, open your hearts with love and see that you have nothing to fear. Release the fear and love yourself! Know that you are important in the overall energy of the earth plane. It is time for you to take your rightful place, as the unique individual you are. You are needed! Your loving, caring, joyful energy is needed, NOW!

Look at yourself and the world through loving, accepting eyes, with an open heart and an open mind. Focus, just for today, on celebrating your life and your earth plane. Send joyful, peaceful thoughts and energy to the whole world! Take the time, today, to stop what you are doing, occasionally, and send your earth plane joyful, loving thoughts, without any expectation, except to share the joy and love that lies within your heart.

Now is the time your earth plane needs these thoughts and this energy! Do not fear, when you do this! Release the fear and concentrate on the love and the joy you wish to project. Call on me and I will assist you in this effort. I am here for you, always, in whatever you wish. Do not look at me in awe, as I am here to serve you in all ways! I will protect you 24/7, if that is what you desire. Just ask and know that I will respond. My protection will, perhaps, release your need to feel tense and fearful. I am here with love, and my strength will protect you from the lower energies. Trust that I am here and that you are protected.

Go forth today and face the world with a joyful heart, celebrating all that is and all that will be. You are protected! You are loved! You are a powerful light-worker. Know this and share your joyful energy! I will protect you, if you "ask"!

I send you love and blessings. I see all the joy and love that lives within you and offer my protection and assistance, to help you be the glorious beings you are. Awaken to your glorious selves.

Eighty-Six

Archangel Zadkiel

Today's message is about forgiveness, compassion and healing. I offer my assistance in helping you release any anger, hurt, or unforgiveness, which you hold in your being. Many of you do not realize that you need to release the anger toward yourself!

You are all open to looking at others with compassion and forgiveness, but you don't realize that you have buried feelings of anger toward yourself. You hold onto hurt and criticism of yourself, for what you consider are failures to meet your own expectations to be fully and completely perfect now. It is time to allow yourself to release these feelings and thoughts! It is time to say, "Enough of the self punishment", in all of its various forms!

You are very adept at punishing yourself and setting the punishment up to look as though it is coming from someone or somewhere else. I say to you, "STOP!" Release the hurt and anger you hold inside toward yourself!

Call on me and I will help you shine a light on those emotions and thoughts that you have kept buried, so that they can be released. This can be done gently and easily, so that you can become aware of what you have buried, but are not drawn in and left feeling depleted. The process can take many forms, but only if you are willing to release these things.

It is time to forgive yourself for everything. It is time to change your focus, from one of self- criticism to one of compassion and understanding. You are perfect just as you are now, but you don't see this.

Each of you is very adept at finding fault in yourself. It is time to change your focus in all ways! I will help you move from your place of unforgiveness toward yourself, to one of awakened understanding and acceptance. This has nothing to do with right or wrong. It has to do with the knowledge that you are all living a process on the earth plane and mistakes and errors are all part of the learning curve.

You need not judge yourselves for anything, as judgment about something doesn't change it. In the process of forgiving yourself, you will release judgments you have held about things you may have said or done. Now is the time to release all of these thoughts and emotions and I will help if you so desire! Allow me to help you release these emotions and from the depth of your soul, feel the peace that is your right. You deserve to be free of these self-defeating thoughts and emotions. You are all bright lights and vibrant energy, waiting to come out from under the shadow of the uncovered beliefs that you do not deserve to be forgiven. Call on me to help you now! Allow the shift in your energy to occur, as you release these lower energies. Be free now and revel in the glory that you are! Awaken, and uncover what you have buried, so that you may release it today. Stop hiding from yourself, there is nothing to fear! Release these beliefs and open to the wonder that is around you and the wonder you can manifest, once you release. Do this today!

There is no reason to hold onto the unforgiveness in your heart, except out of fear of the unknown. I say to you, "When you release these feelings, a new, more peaceful and joyful existence will awaken in you!" Fear not, for you have much joy ahead of you.

I bring you love, joy, peace and healing now. You are all worthy and you have done nothing that can't be forgiven. Allow the forgiveness to fill your hearts and minds, so that you may be free to awaken, more completely, to the peace and joy within.

Eighty-Seven

Ishtar

Today I come before you to offer healing on all levels. Healing is holistic and, therefore, to be truly healed, you heal on all levels. I offer my assistance and shine the light of love on you to protect you from the lower energies.

At times you may allow the lower energies to influence you and affect your life. Call on me to help you release these energies and step into my light, as I surround you and send love to you. Know that you may call on me at any time to release you from the lower energies. Do not allow the energies, such as fear, anger, jealousy and others to take root!

When you begin to feel these feelings, take the time to understand what is happening. Bring these feelings into the light, so that once they have been exposed, they can be released. Do not bury them, as when you do, they will only fester like an old wound; and when they finally emerge into the light, it may become worse than the original emotion. These feelings do exist within you, but they can be mere irritants, rather than all-consuming feelings. I will assist you in releasing all of these feelings, just ask.

Know that you need not be concerned with many of these

lower energies, if you focus your attention on the divine within. You may experience the beginning of the feelings, but you can choose to release them and move your focus into another direction. You have the choice! Do not deny the emotions, but do not let them remain in your being for any length of time, as the sooner they are released, the easier it will be to release them in the future.

Practice accepting that you may be feeling any of these lower energies. Bring the feeling into your consciousness, which is the same as bringing it into the light; then have the observer part of you, look at the energy it takes to retain these feelings, without judgment. Now you may choose to stay in the feeling or to release it; again, without judgment. You have the choice.

It is my honor to help you release these feelings, regardless of how long they have been a part of your life. Ask and I will come to surround you with light, fill you with love, and release these lower energies. You make the decision and it can be done gently and easily, without pain. You do not have to relive old situations to release them. I will help you do this! I am honored to serve you in this way.

I send you love, light and offer my assistance in releasing any and all lower energies, from anywhere in your being. Be free today! Share joy and love, releasing everything that keeps you depressed and stuck. Start the process today.

Eighty-Eight

Mother Mary

I come to you today to surround you with unconditional love. It is a time for you to rest in this love, for soon you will be moving at a more rapid pace than you have been. Take today and allow me to surround and fill you with the love that is already within. Feel my love! Know that you need do nothing, to receive this love. Open your heart and mind to this love. Accept that this love is for you, and you deserve it. Know that I wish to enfold you in my loving embrace, as mothers do with all children throughout the ages. You are my children and I love you! Live, for now, in peace and love!

Rest in the knowledge that you are safe and loved. You are in my arms and protected with my love and understanding. I send you compassion and healing. I surround you with the love and compassion that I send into the world. Live in this feeling, today! Feel the peace and the love fill your heart. Feel yourself relax into this love and finally, find peace. This love I send is for you and about you. It is healing and peaceful and will help you to rest and to believe in yourself.

I am always here for you, in all ways. You can call on me and I will take you in my arms and hold you until your heart relaxes, in peace. Do not hesitate, or fear that you may be taking me from something more important. Like all the angels and ascended masters, I can be in many places at once. You are important and deserve to be loved! Call on me at any time and I will come!

You are in my thoughts and prayers. Let me bring you my love and help you release your fears, opening to compassion and understanding. Accept that this is so, and then feel how, with accepting what I offer, you will experience your own peace and compassion. I am here for you!

I send you blessings, love and compassion. Accept that this is where you are, today. Be with me and let me fill your being with love and peace.

Eighty-Nine

Serapis Bey

I come today to talk to you about maintaining your connection with Spirit. When you feel disconnected, it is because you are rushing around, focused on things that need to be done and as your mind and body race around, you forget to connect. Know that you are always connected. You just don't hear the guidance, as you are not listening.

To hear the guidance, you need to take the time to quiet yourself and listen. Spirit is with you always, and the guidance you seek is always available. Just take even five minutes to sit quietly and focus within. By doing so, this will help you in many ways, the major one being connecting with Spirit. The divine lies within you, as you.

Know that you have the wisdom to make choices, already existing within. Call on me and I will help move you along your chosen path. I will assist you in gaining perspective and hearing the wisdom from within. As you listen to the guidance, you will know that this information is directing you toward a higher goal along your path.

Do not fear that you are incapable of reaching the goal. Know that what you can imagine, you can do! The guidance you need to progress toward you goal is already within. Now is the time to take the time to listen to that which is within. Reconnect daily and feel yourself expand and rise up into a different vibration. Your well being is important to all, as you are an integral part of the whole. Know you are loved and that the guidance you desire is within.

I send you love and blessings. I offer my support in shifting your focus and your vibration. I await your request.

Ninety

Aine

Today I stress living from lightness and joy. I see all of you living your lives on the earth plane with such seriousness. I ask that you call on me to lighten your load and to strengthen your courage and faith, as you set about your mission and purpose. You are important and your mission is important, but be aware that it does no good to take yourself so seriously that you cannot hear others speak! You look at your life so seriously that at times, it all becomes too much to bear.

Know that you will accomplish just as much by living your life from a lighter position. Play music, sing, skip, laugh and share joy; all of which will help you on your path and with your mission. Call on me to lighten your load! I will repeat a statement that many of you are familiar with, in this regard: "Angels can fly, because they take themselves lightly!"

By releasing some of your seriousness, you can open yourself to greater understanding and growth. You are all here for a divine mission and life purpose, but it will happen, more easily and with less stress, if you lighten up.

Now is the time to focus on the lightness and contentment you all feel, when you are surrounded by others of like mind and heart. I will help you light the fire of passion in your life, but I will do so with a lightness of touch, so that what you are passionate about will bring joy, instead of stress.   K n o w that there is no right or wrong way to approach your mission. Focus on the joy, focus on the passion you feel when you are totally involved in your life and live from that position! You are supported in all ways, every day.

Know that you are not alone and release the burden. Approach your life purpose with passion and a light heart, trusting that you will be guided toward your mission and what you are here to do will happen with ease and success. I will help you with this!

I send you love, support and offer my help in firing up the passion in your life.

Ninety-One

Archangel Michael

Today I offer my services to you for courage, protection and encouragement. I am here to encourage you, in all ways, to listen to your inner guides and take the steps, which will move you in the complete direction of your life purpose. I will be here to help you with the courage to do this, regardless of the reaction of others. You are all on the brink of this change. You are all standing at the precipice and yet, there appears to be something holding you back. I offer my assistance in helping you to take that step. You may call it a leap, and for some it is a leap, but Now is the time to do it!

I see the divine in each of you. I know what you are capable of creating and bringing to the earth plane. Trust what you are hearing in your mind and heart! Know that regardless of your beliefs to the contrary, you are all magnificent beings with much to offer to the world around you and beyond!

You have all gone through many changes in the past. All of the changes have had an impact on who you are in the physical plane, but beneath it all, you are still divine! Spirit is calling you, to take your place in the creative plan. You are being called, to acknowledge that you have a life purpose and now is the time to follow that path, without doubt or reservation! I am here to protect you and to assist you with your courage. Be not afraid, for you are protected and loved, and all of your wants and needs will be supplied. Know that the universe is abundant and you are not being called into a life of poverty. When you follow your life purpose, you open to giving, serving and receiving. You are all very adept at giving and serving. Now is the time to also receive! I offer my assistance in providing you with the courage to ask for compensation for your services. Money is energy and therefore, I offer this idea. When you offer your services and you receive money for said services, this is an energy exchange. Take the risk! Follow your guidance from within and then ask for the money!

I realize many of you are asking yourselves, "How can I speak of such mundane things?" Well, I tell you that it is important that I speak of this, as part of the hesitation in following your inner guidance is the fear that you will be heading into a life of poverty. I wish to allay this fear and I wish to emphasize that prosperity can be found not only in the work you are currently doing, but in following your life purpose.

Open your hearts and minds! Step along the path you committed to before you entered the earth plane! Know in your hearts, that you have all the support you need to fulfill your commitment. I will help you, now!

I will help you create opportunities to bring in the prosperity, if you will take the risk and renew the commitment to your "life purpose." Now is the time! Now is when you are needed! It starts with a small step and then, an open heart and mind! Open to the opportunities that await you! Open, and be receptive to all that Spirit wishes to give. I will protect you and give you courage. Now is the time to take the first step, even if all you do is to say Yes to what you are being called to do.

I offer my love, my protection and my assistance in every phase of your awakening to who you really are.

Ninety-Two

Metatron

I come today to encourage you and help you with the motivation to follow your divine mission and life purpose. You sit in fear of rejection and of the unknown, and I come to offer you all of our support!

I come to speak for those of us in the other realms, who see you take a tentative step forward and then, hesitate. We see that you know, in your hearts, what you are to do and what will fill your soul and yet, stay in your current place, thinking that by staying there you will be safe. I say to you, "Take the steps necessary, to follow your divine guidance!" Sit and listen to the guidance from within and then "follow the ideas and inspirations", as they come to you. Know that you are fully supported in this. Release the fears that hold you back!

Know that you have all the tools necessary to do what you desire. This does not mean that you won't continue to learn, but it does mean that you need not fear being unprepared or unqualified. You are all ready to do what you came here to do. Call on me, and I will assist you with ideas for taking the first steps. When you call on me, understand that you will hear these ideas in your head and from the mouths of others!

Someone will say something, and it will inspire you to do something you hadn't thought of.

You are all ready to go forth! Do not fear that you will falter. Listen to your guides and then, take action! Call on all of us for support, as we are here for you. You are never alone, and there are many of us who stand waiting for your call! Accept our offer and follow our guidance, then watch as the things that you are capable of creating, manifest before your eyes!

If we could take each of you and change your beliefs immediately, we would; but you have free will, and this includes the freedom to live in fear, clinging to beliefs which no longer serve you.

Be open to receiving our help! Know that nothing is more important to us than assisting you in every area of your life.

The earth plane has undergone numerous changes and now the atmosphere is in place for you to let your knowledge come forth. Be not afraid, for you are loved and supported in all that you do. Be not afraid that you are being judged. We wish only the very best for you and I am here to tell you, "We are here to serve!" Call on us to help you through your transitions and in all daily life, where we can make things easier. We say to you that, "You need not struggle so much!" Ask for the help and then, know that we will respond! Just stay alert for the answers and help.

I leave you with blessings, love and my support, as well as the support of everyone in the other realms. Claim your right to this support, now.

Ninety-Three

Archangel Jeremiel

I come to offer my help in guiding you in the steps to take to follow your life mission. I can assist you in your dreams and help you to have prophetic dreams about the future of your planet and your life. Call on me and not only will I provide help with dreams about the future, but I will help guide you in the steps necessary to fulfill the dream. You are ready for this, now!

You have all opened your hearts and now is the time to listen to what you hear and envision for yourself and others. You are capable of manifesting your dreams and the dreams of the future may come true. I do add a caution that, "Although I can provide prophetic dreams, you still have free will, and decisions you make can affect the outcome of all prophecies!"

Know that you are powerful beings and that when you cooperate in a group and profess the same intentions, you can affect the vibration and energy around you and it will have a ripple effect. Know that whatever energy you send out just by yourself can have a ripple effect. Call on me to assist you, now!

Pay attention to your dreams to uncover the information I have assisted you in discovering. If you are uncomfortable with seeing the future, you may just call on me to help you with the things you need to do to have a fulfilling future.

You are all gifted and I ask you to approach your future with fearlessness and hope. Your earth plane is in transition and if you all do your part, the future of your planet and your world can be glorious. I send you love and hope for each day.

Ninety-Four

Archangel Ariel

I come before you to speak about your role in helping the environment. As you know, there is a delicate balance that is always in play. It is important to be aware of how you treat the environment and to help to keep the balance. I do not require that you devote your lives to the environment and all of the beings who inhabit your oceans, forests, lakes, etc., but, I do request that you not pollute, even small ways!

I ask you to think about doing your part to maintain the balance in your earth's nature. As you know, the trees and plants help to maintain the correct amount of oxygen necessary for humans to breathe. Everything works together in harmony, to allow all that is on earth to continue to grow. Now is a time when all efforts are needed to maintain the balance. Now is the time when even small things done to help the environment are appreciated and needed. I am here to help you; but you can help, by being aware of your surroundings and the nature that soothes your soul. Today take the time to be in nature; acknowledge the beauty that surrounds you! Wherever you live on the earth plane, there is nature. Enjoy it today! Walk in it, sit in it, and just be in nature today!

Show your gratitude for all that nature offers, by picking up trash, or watering a plant, or hugging a tree. I will provide guidance, to show how you can assist in maintaining the balance of nature. Remember, that when you help maintain the balance in the environment, you are helping yourself to have healthy, energizing atmospheres in which to live. The wood nymphs, fairies, elves and all of the other beings who make the natural places their home, wish to express their appreciation for all that you do, so keep your eyes open and you may be delighted with what you observe!

I send you my blessings and my gratitude for anything you can do to help the environment.

Ninety-Five

Kuan Ti

It is important that you are all aware that the constant effort on the part of governments to instill fear in everyone is affecting the vibration of your earth plane. I say this to emphasize the importance, at this time, for all of you to concentrate and focus on love and healing, rather than fear. If you move into the fear energy and you live from that place, you increase the fear vibration, rather than reduce it.

Now is the time to ensure that your focus is one of peace and love! If you find it difficult to change your focus to one of love and understanding, call on me and I will help you. I wish to emphasize that all the energy is needed, at this time, to focus on love, so that the fear can be released and dissipate. To live in the constant state of fear is harmful and does not accomplish anything. Listen to your inner-knowing and follow that, rather than the information that is being broadcast by the political leaders.

I am here to help you come from a place of love. Take back your power and continue to live in love! Allow those of us from the other realms to assist you now, by supporting and protecting you.

Know that you have the power to affect change. When you focus on loving energy, you affect those around you in a loving way and this, in turn, increases the loving energy. You have the power to choose how you wish to focus your day and how you wish to be. Take your power back! Do not allow others to influence your feelings and choices.

Listen to what is being said, but understand that what is right for someone else is not necessarily right for you! It is time that you not argue about who is right and who is wrong. Take the time to understand things from another's perspective. Work to reach a consensus with each other and send this thought to others who are in conflict. The need to be right does not bring solutions to problems. You must work together to come to an understanding of differing points of view, and then find the solution, via discussion and compassion. Now you are needed to use your power to focus on love and understanding, so that when the masses center their focus on peace, it will change the energy.

Fear begets more fear, and when you come from fear, you need to protect and preserve your position with control. As you know, there is only one person you can control and that is you; therefore, operating out of fear and attempting to control others will only create chaos! Choose love and release fear. I will help and I await your call.

I send support and encouragement to all. Love, peace and understanding can lead to a more peaceful place for all.

Ninety-Six

Archangel Chamuel

I am here to offer my services to aid you in making life choices. I can assist you when you doubt that you are following the correct course for you. I can help you lay a sound foundation for the choices that you make. Whatever you are questioning, know that going inside will give you direction. Listen to that which comes from within. You are your greatest source of information and inspiration, when you come from your highest self. You will know that which will fill your soul and give you the greatest joy, if you will but listen.

Many of you hear the information and then, doubt what you are hearing. You listen to the opinions of others, without thinking that you are each individuals; and what is the correct course of action for you, is not necessarily the correct course of action for another. Do not be led into a course of action that does not resonate with you! You need to pay attention to that small voice within, which has never steered you in the wrong direction (when you have listened to it and followed its advice). I see many of you listening, then taking a small step in the direction and then backing off and going an entirely different direction, because you know it and it feels safe. I say to you,

"Now is the time to follow that which is coming from within, rather than that which is coming from the outside!"

Now is the time that you are being encouraged to take the risk, which in our opinion is not a risk, as the outcome can only help you along the way to your life mission.

Know that even if you falter, you are like a comet that is directed by a computer; for every error, there is an automatic correction, so that the goal can be reached. Take the step. Listen to your higher self follow the guidance and direction. Release the fear and fly! Now is the time for you to soar! Call on me to help you with the choices. I will come immediately and assist you!

You are reading this and therefore, are open to taking the risk. Others may disagree with your choices. That's OK, as the choices you make are yours, not theirs. Let each follow his or her own path, without judgment or condemnation. Follow the guidance of your inner-self and let your life take wings! Now is the time and I will support you, as will all from the other realms. Do it now! Open your ears, your mind, your heart and soar like an eagle.

I support you in your choices and will assist in establishing firm foundations for everything in your life. Blessings and love as you release the fear and doubt to move into the very life you committed to living, prior to coming to the earth plane.

Ninety-Seven

Dana

∽

Now is the time to acknowledge that you are all royalty! I know that we have discussed this before, but I come today to reiterate it. Take a moment out of your day and focus your mind and being on the royalty that you are. Surround yourself in the royal color of purple or deep crimson. Center your being and bring this light inside you, filling all your cells and all of your chakras with the color. Let the color permeate your entire being and then be in the energy for even a few minutes.

Allow me to cover you with a royal cloak and give you gifts fit for royalty. Open to receive all that you wish in your life. Now is the time for you to receive! As royalty, you deserve the best! Shed your doubts and accept, with grace, all that is offered. It is time to just say, "Thank you", without qualifications of any kind.

I sense discomfort as you read this. Fear not, for I speak the truth about you. Release the beliefs of unworthiness, if only for five minutes. Release all your training about being sinners; you have learned this lesson too well. This is a term designed to control you. Let it go now, for it does not serve you or the earth plane. You are all born of Spirit and, therefore, are filled with light. Release the dust around your light and let it shine forth now!

The important thing for today is that you accept all help offered! It is time for you to know that you have all the support you need and to accept the help offered. I am honored to serve you in any way I can and I will help you with divine magic and manifestation. Know that it is right for you to receive prosperity. Call on me and I will help you receive with joy, peace and without guilt.

Today take the step and receive, as you wish others to receive gifts that you offer. It is time for you to be who you are and let the divine, which is within, shine forth and receive.

I send you love and blessings and surround you with the royal cloak, which will help you feel that you deserve to receive all that is offered.

Ninety-Eight

Archangel Raguel

I come to offer my services in any way you need help. I am capable of helping you in all areas of your life, therefore, if you are unsure who to call on for assistance, just call on me and I will help directly, or whisper in your ear who else you might call on. You are not alone! You need not struggle through your lives on earth; there are easier ways of awakening rather than through suffering.

I see most of you struggling through your lives on the earth plane, when there is help awaiting your call.

All of you are capable of manifesting what you desire, but you sabotage yourselves, unconsciously. Awaken to your abilities and what is your birthright! Know that you can experience life on the earth plane from a position of peace, rather than pain. You need not do everything alone! It is not necessary to struggle with pain and sorrow, to grow. It is not necessary to do everything yourself, when you have angels and ascended masters awaiting your request for help. Your path through life can be made easier if you will just ask for help and then accept it in all its various forms.

We come to you in a variety of ways. There are times when

we work through other humans, so do not block all information you receive from others. Just check in with your higher-self before taking it at face value. Know that your life can be easier and that you have help on many levels. I repeat what we have said before, "Be open to receiving help!" Know that you deserve help.

Check your beliefs in every area of your life. Release the fear and doubt! Come from a place of love and light, both for yourself and your fellow humans. Show yourself the love you wish to give to others. Give yourself the same compassion and acceptance you, so readily, give to others. I am here to help!

Allow me to ease your burdens, so you may know peace and joy. Watch what happens to those around you, when you change from pain to joy. See how others blossom, when you allow your burdens to be released and you approach life with love, laughter and joy.

Know that with focus and intention, you can change your thinking and your life. Give to yourself all the love you share with others, knowing that the more you care for yourself, the more you will have to give. Approach this day filled with love and awe for yourself. Show yourself gratitude for being who you are! Just for today, love yourself unconditionally and open your heart to joy and laughter. Release your burdens and sing!

I send you joy, laughter and help in every area of your life.

Ninety-Nine

Diana

⁓

It is time to shine. It is time for you to be who you are and release any fears of rejection, or ridicule. You are grand and glorious beings and are needed now. I offer my support in this effort. Fear not, as your wisdom is valuable and needed. Acknowledge the divine within and shine! Let the very being within shine forth today.

Express yourself fully, without regard to the opinions of others. If you feel like dancing, or singing, or laughing, then do so now! Do not hold back. Focus your thoughts on the reality within and release your daily concerns, if only for a minute. Release your burdens and worries! Release your fears and doubts!

You have come into this earth plane to share your gifts now is the time! Do not hold back anything you wish to share. Be like the lights you see around you in the form of the moon, the stars and the sun; they shine their light for all to see! It is time for you to do the same, so that others may let their light shine!

I realize that many of you are afraid to let others see who you really are, but I will assist you in this. Call on me and I will help you with the courage to live authentically, from your heart. In living from your heart, you may surprise some and encourage others. It matters not how you are perceived, as it is important for the energy of the earth plane that you accept your rightful place in the world. Acknowledge and share your gifts! Do not hide them under a basket, hoping not to be noticed. You may choose to stay hidden, but by doing so you fail to fulfill your divine mission and that is part of the reason you came into this life at this time!

Know that within you lies untapped strength, wisdom, information and love, which can be shared. Know that there is no one else who can take your place, as each of you has unique gifts and talents to offer. It is true all are connected and you can operate as one; yet, at the same time you are unique and as such, your gifts are a necessary part of the whole. Be not afraid, for we will support you and you will receive support from those on the physical plane as well. Be open to sharing and receiving, as is your due. Today is the day! Take a step in the direction your soul is calling. Now is the time! Do not hesitate! Be all you can be with love, lightness and laughter in your being. Take the chance and live your life as you desire.

I send you support, love and protection for everything you do.

One Hundred

Archangel Jeremiel

I come to honor and help you today with decisions and guidance. I see many of you have an understanding of your life purpose, but no idea how to get started working it. Call on me, and I will help give you the steps necessary to further your mission.

You are each on the edge of doing what is important to you and the world in which you live. Know that you contribute every day, whether you realize it or not. You impact those around you and beyond, but if you are unsure of what the next steps are, then you can call on me and I will assist you. I will come to you in your dreams if you desire, or during times of meditation, to offer suggestions of a prophetic nature about your future and the future of the world in which you live. I will guide you along the path, should you choose to ask for my help. Again I repeat what others have said before me, "Listen, and you will hear my response!"

It is important, at this point, for me to mention that no matter what I say, the choice to follow my advice is still yours! You have the power to make the choices. Nothing is written in stone and although I can provide information about the future, it is still your choice! The things you intend and what you do, affect all outcomes in your life. You make the decision to act, think or feel; the choice is yours and therefore, you create the outcome!

I can assist you in bringing about a more fulfilling outcome if you are unsure of what to do, but you need to listen and follow my guidance! I am here to support you and guide you to the most fulfilling future, if you ask and listen, and then follow my suggestions. Know that I will be by your side during the time you are following my guidance and it will provide you with the courage to follow your dream. Ask for help, take the leap and reap the rewards!

I send you my support and guidance as you awaken, more fully, into who you are and why you have chose to be here now.

One Hundred One

Maitreya

You all know me as I have spoken before, but as a reminder, I am known as the "Laughing Buddha." I see much sadness around today and much seriousness, as you all get caught up in your own troubles and concerns on the physical plane.

I know you believe that these are real and that you are totally involved in these troubles, but you do not have to carry these burdens alone. As you have heard many times, the angels and ascended masters are here to help you in everything. It does not matter whether you consider the situation large or small, they are here for you! I offer my help and guidance to take yourselves and your life less seriously.

I know that you are all aware of the basic precepts of letting go and not worrying, however, it helps to repeat things that may help to ease your burdens and worry. Change your focus, now! Shift your focus to something that will make you smile, or even laugh. Do not get caught up in the story that you create, with worry!

You can change the energy around a situation, if you will only change the way you look at it. You can create a more positive outcome, when you change your focus and your energy.

Worry solves nothing and only continues to focus your energy on the negative, or an outcome you do not wish for.

One way to change your focus is to hum a tune or sing a song. Music can have a powerful affect on where you put your energy. Music is a powerful tool for manifesting and changing the energy around you. Humming or singing will change not only your vibration but, the vibration in the situation; this brings to mind a song from an old movie (I know many of you think that we are above the earthly pleasures of movies, but we do indulge).

Getting back to the song, (perhaps some of you will remember it from your childhood) the song says, "Whenever you feel afraid, just whistle a happy tune and then you won't feel so alone." Think about this and do it; you will be amazed how it changes your focus! Know that I tell you this, because much of what you worry about is out of your control. The only thing you can control is you and your attitude, so ask for help and release the heavy burden that you carry.

Know that you face every day with the intention to do the very best that you can; and then, live each moment as it comes! Laughter is a tonic that will keep you centered in the present moment. Perhaps you can only release a small amount of the worry, then smile! That is fine, as even a smile will move you from worry to living in the present moment. Know that life is a banquet and as you experience it, you will discern which experiences you wish to put on your plate to taste.

I leave you with this blessing: Share laughter, joy and music to brighten your day, as you work through the experiences of your life. Lighten your load and your life, by asking for help and know the request will be answered. Remember, whenever you are in fear and worry, just whistle a happy tune.

ABOUT KATHLEEN

Kathleen grew up in Minneapolis, Minnesota. She has been involved in spiritual exploration for most of her life, although she wasn't aware that it was spiritual in nature. Throughout her career, which began with social work, followed by management positions in business, she searched for some type of work that would incorporate her quest for understanding, her intuitive abilities and her desire to help people.

In 1984, while living in Los Angeles, she became actively involved with the Healing Arts Center in Woodland Hills, California, taking classes and then teaching meditation, spiritual development, Feng Shui, crystals and alternative methods of healing. Kathleen began channeling in 1994.

Kathleen is an experienced trans-channel and has been offering metaphysical training and personal consultations in spiritual exploration, angels and meditation to the public since 1990, and has students and clients across the nation. She has studied with master teachers and is a Reiki Practitioner, Certified Energy Healer, and an Angel Therapy Practitioner and Professional Spiritual Teacher certified by Dr. Doreen Virtue, PhD. (www.angeltherapy.com).

In both her seminars and private practice, she offers the use of multiple modalities. Kathleen does both private and public channeling from the angels and other enlightened beings.